THEY STILL DRAW PICTURES

CHILDREN'S ART IN WARTIME
FROM THE SPANISH CIVIL WAR TO KOSOVO

ANTHONY L. GEIST AND PETER N. CARROLL
FOREWORD BY ROBERT COLES

UNIVERSITY OF ILLINOIS PRESS
URBANA AND CHICAGO

Publication of this book was supported by a grant from
the University of Washington Graduate School Fund for
Excellence and Innovation

©2002 by the Board of Trustees of the University of Illinois
All rights reserved
Manufactured in Canada
1 2 3 4 5 C P 5 4 3 2 1

♾ This book is printed on acid-free paper

Published in conjunction with an exhibition curated by Anthony L. Geist and
Peter N. Carroll for the Abraham Lincoln Brigade Archives and the Mandeville
Special Collections Library at the University of California at San Diego.

Library of Congress Cataloging-in-Publication Data
Geist, Anthony L., 1945 –
They still draw pictures : children's art in wartime from the Spanish Civil War
to Kosovo / Anthony L. Geist and Peter N. Carroll ; foreword by Robert Coles
p. cm.
ISBN 0-252-02716-7 (cloth : alk. paper)
ISBN 0-252-07026-7 (paper : alk. paper)
1. Children's art. 2. War in art. 3. Spain—History—Civil War,
1936–1939—Art and the war. I. Carroll, Peter N. II. Title.
N352.G38 2002
750'.83—dc21   2001002478

CONTENTS

ACKNOWLEDGMENTS **5**

FOREWORD
CHILDREN'S ART IN WARTIME **6**
BY ROBERT COLES

INTRODUCTION **10**
BY ANTHONY L. GEIST

ESSAY
CHILDREN OF THE SPANISH CIVIL WAR **13**
BY ANTHONY L. GEIST

        BEFORE **26**
        WAR **30**
        DISPLACEMENT **36**
        CAMPS **42**
        PEACE **48**

COLOR PLATES **53**

INTERVIEW **76**

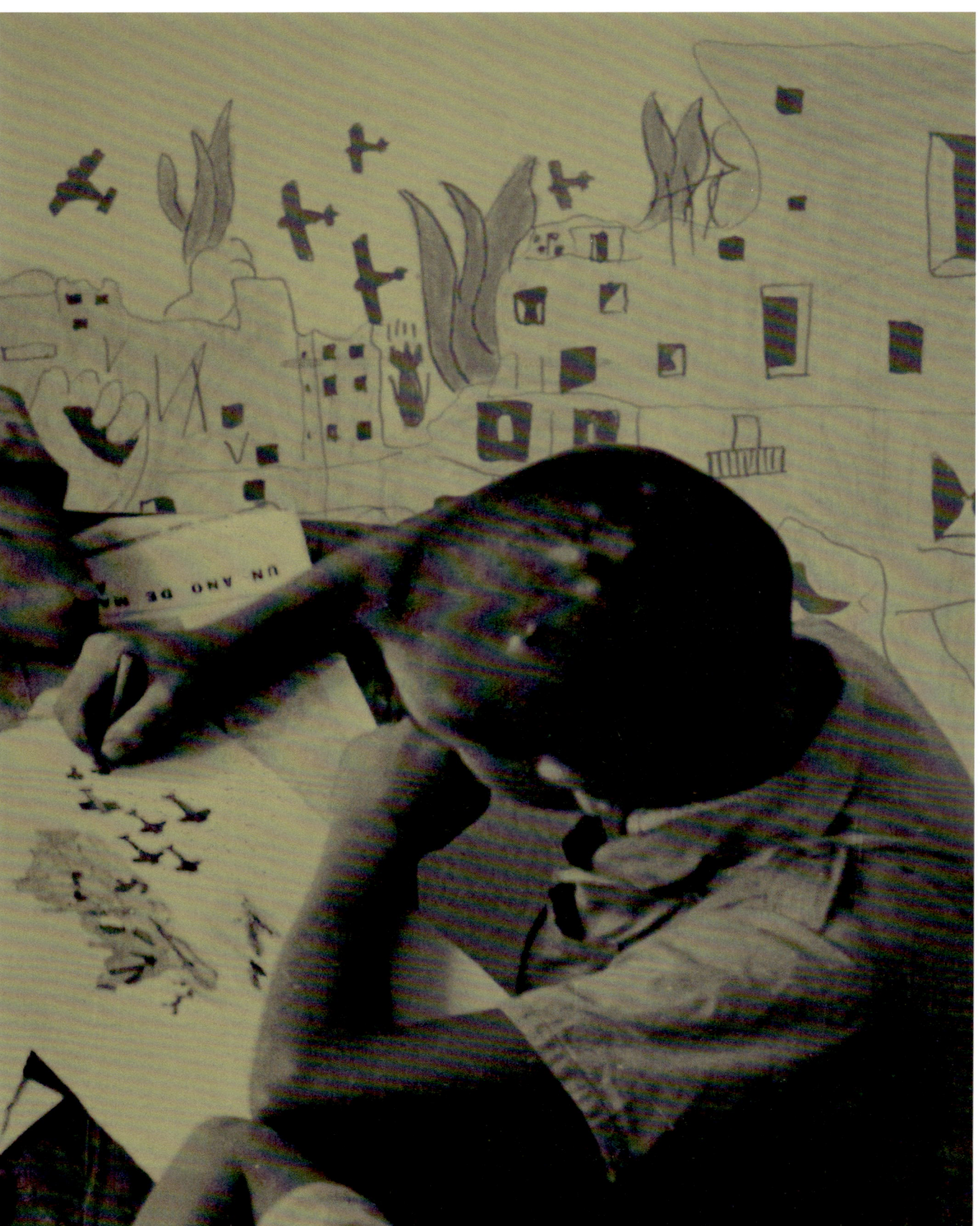

5
ACKNOWLEDGMENTS

The authors would like to acknowledge the many people and institutions who, in different capacities, made this book and exhibition possible. Our gratitude to:

Richard Bermack, Emilio Cassinello, Lynda Claassen, Montserrat Domínguez, Jim Fernández, Jeannette Ferrary, Denis Fitzpatrick, Jennifer Geist, Anci Koppel, Virginia Malbin, José Moreno, Cary Nelson, Julia Newman, Miguel Ángel Nieto, Abe Osheroff, Fraser Ottanelli, Antonio Ramos Gascón, Perry and Gladys Rosenstein, Sol Sender, Bill Susman, Fredda Weiss, Trudy White and Julián Zugazagoitia. Special thanks to Alicia Díez, José Moreno de la Puerta, and Alfonso Ortuño for agreeing to be interviewed for this book.

MATERIAL SUPPORT WAS PROVIDED BY: Paul Blanc, the Consulate General of Spain (New York), the Estate of Isabel Johnson Hiss, Program for Cultural Cooperation Between Spain's Ministry of Culture and U.S. Universities, the Puffin Foundation Ltd., the Sonya Staff Foundation, University of Washington Graduate School Fund for Excellence and Innovation, Utrecht Art Supplies.

WE WOULD ESPECIALLY LIKE TO THANK THE FOLLOWING PEOPLE AND INSTITUTIONS FOR PERMISSION TO EXHIBIT AND REPRODUCE DRAWINGS AND PHOTOS: Cornell Capa (International Center of Photography), Dr. Alexander Matthews (heir to Martha Gellhorn), Kathleen King, the Biblioteca Nacional (Madrid), the Frente Zapatista de Liberación Nacional (Mexico), the Hoover Institution for War, Peace and Revolution (Stanford University), the Butler Library (Columbia University), the Israel Museum (Jerusalem), the National Japanese American Historical Society (San Francisco), the Middle East Children's Alliance (Oakland), the San Francisco International Children's Art Museum, the Terezin Memorial Museum (Czechoslovakia).

THIS BOOK IS DEDICATED TO: Jennifer, Sophie, and Rosie: "I love you and my heart is simple" (ALG). Eva and Ben: artists for a peaceful age (PNC).

FOREWORD
CHILDREN'S ART IN WARTIME

BY ROBERT COLES

While learning to work with boys and girls as a physician, I had to learn how to communicate with them—ask them questions, listen to their questions, understand what they had in mind, even as I had to figure out how to convey my own mind's thoughts, worries, concerns, hopes. By the time I became a pediatrician, I was doing fairly well in the numerous conversations that took place between me and the ailing or quite sick children who were my patients and whom I kept trying to assist medically on a hospital ward or in clinics. In particular, though, I remember one of the children, who had been hospitalized with a severe case of pneumonia and who had little to say on admission and thereafter, no matter that he was nine years old, in the fourth grade, and a good, outspoken student there—so his parents had told me after I first examined him in the emergency ward of the Children's Hospital in Boston.

7

CHILDREN'S ART IN WARTIME

For the first days of his stay with us on the infectious disease ward I kept trying to have a reasonably brief, friendly conversation with that youngster, John by first name, but Jack to his friends and family alike. One morning, at the end of ward rounds, led by a visitor, a revered physician known for his ability to get on well with children as well as take accurate estimate of what bothered them, I was asked by our regular attending pediatrician about John's "manner"—the use of that word was a bit odd, I recall thinking right away. My face must have registered a certain perplexity, hence a brief spell of silence as I struggled for the sentences of a reply. Then I heard this: "He seemed like a quiet boy. Has he said much to you?" More silence on my part as I tried to come up with spoken language, to no avail—and in no time, a further comment by our attending pediatrician: "For a long while, I had a great deal of trouble talking with certain children; they'd stare and say not a word—often stare away. What to do? An elder pediatrician took me aside one day and suggested I try drawing with the children. I had no idea how to draw myself, nor had I any idea of how to proceed—ask these boys and girls in the hospital to draw pictures! But I learned a lot from the ones I did ask to draw!"

That was that—he moved along from bed to bed, and we young doctors with him. In no time my mind was all taken up with medical matters, and the idea of asking children to draw pictures was well put aside in my thinking. But the next day another older pediatrician, who had been there on rounds that morning, stopped me near the ward station and echoed what had been said. He told me how interesting it can be for doctors to look at the drawings and paintings children make—and, he added, for us to hear what those young people have to say about what they have done with crayons or pencils and pens or paint brushes. He took me to his office and showed me the drawings and paintings of his youthful patients, told me about all of them, their ages, their pediatric problems, and the remarks they'd made—what they'd pictured and, often enough, the stories by them that went with their artistic efforts (all of that written down on pieces of paper that he'd attached to this or that child's portrait of a person or self-portrait or landscape or building rendered—a house, a school, a hospital).

Now I was quite stirred. I had taken many art history courses in college; and no small matter, my mother was an amateur artist, even as my wife, Jane, would one day teach schoolchildren in all their subjects, including a "period" devoted to "art"—held in a classroom "studio" dedicated to the encouragement of drawing and painting. The long and short of it: I began, back then, a clinical life with children that would last decades and that would include, significantly, a continuing interest in how those boys and girls responded through pictorial representation to the world they all the time experienced. What a pediatrician suggested to me soon enough became what I did as a young child psychiatrist. Indeed, I think it fair to say, my decision to pursue training in child psychiatry was prompted by the kind of pediatric work I began doing as I sat with children, asked them to draw or paint, and afterward talked with them about their work—we were, that way, getting close to their mind's life, its worries and expectations and yearnings, its memories of the past and hopes for the future. Such meetings, casual and fitted into a busy pediatric ward life, eventually became part of an abiding interest in children's artwork as an expression of their emotional world and their intellectual life. As my work moved from hospitals and clinics to neighborhoods, as I began to connect my working life to children initiating school desegregation in the 1960s South, to the children who lived in relatively obscure or impoverished parts of America or in countries abroad, I found myself constantly paying attention to what I could learn from all those youngsters through a scrutiny, with their help, of their drawn or painted pictures.

No wonder two important psychoanalytic teachers of mine would want to regard closely the visual work of those children—would encourage me to focus my research work through a constant notice given to what youths convey to us, reveal to us, when they put on paper a whole subject matter that has great meaning to them. Here speaking is Erik H. Erikson, himself an artist before he became a distinguished psychoanalyst, historian, and biographer: "Every night, as adults we show ourselves pictures and tie them to words, to talk—that is what a dream is. We wake up after our dreams to remember a sequence of pictures and some language we spoke through the individuals who appeared in our sleeping minds. I remember when I'd tell Anna Freud what I'd dreamt. [She was his training analyst, and her father, Sigmund Freud, helped her understand her various analysands' dreams, including Erikson's, when she reported them to him.] Miss Freud would listen and try to make sense of what I remembered; and sometimes, she'd encourage me—well, prod me—to go further and tell her more of what happened. She'd put it this way: 'Tell me what you saw last night in your dreams, as well as what you said, or had other people say to you.' Then she'd stop, and I'd hear a bit of a lecture: 'Dreams are the mind's story-telling pictures—we "show and tell" through the dreams we have and try to hold onto the next morning. That is why I ask children to draw—that way, they tell me what is on their minds by sketching the message on paper.' I can hear her saying that, and I knew her father had a hand in her thinking that way!"

9

CHILDREN'S ART IN WARTIME

As Erikson and I would look at the pictures children had made for me, in the course of those many meetings, in homes, in schools, in neighborhood settings such as libraries or playgrounds, he would often become the art critic as well as the child psychoanalyst. He would notice colors chosen for this or that person, place, thing; he would observe the way a child filled up a given space and, of course, the way people were represented—their facial expressions, the clothes given them, their arms and legs and torsos as they got set down. The suns and clouds of a daytime sky or, alternatively, the moons and stars that told of the night also interested him, as did the land's given possessions, its grass or trees or roads or buildings. ("So much there, in that thin stretch of land," he once said, looking at a particular child's picture of his backyard). All in all, he was taking very seriously what he saw, courtesy of a child's willingness to use crayons as a means of setting down, putting forth what his mind wanted to show, bring to observable life. Once that lad referred to the "artwork" he did as "crayola magic," his vivid way of saying a lot, actually: those crayons used on paper, in an hour's time, gave visual expression to, gave a kind of permanence to, his life's interests (some of them preoccupations) as they sought the narrative opportunity crayons and paper allow—the magical transformation into drawn or painted pictures of passing reveries, of remembered lessons learned, of felt attachments or disappointments, all kept under wraps one minute, allowed entry into awareness the next. During an American visit (1968) Anna Freud told a roomful of us what she had confided to Erik Erikson in the small room that was her Vienna office: "When a child draws a picture, the watching adult world is being told and taught something. That picture is a day-dream: an artist has converted mental life into a picture's life (after all, its meaning and story, its content and its intent, come from a person's mind—a kind of human expressiveness artists all the time and all over the world have given us)!"

Here, then, are some of those artists—young, but no less drawn to pictures than the rest of us who visit museums, look at pictures worked into books or hung on walls. A drawing or a painting is a soul's message eagerly sought by us watchful onlookers. Whether the artist be grown up or a boy or a girl, the point is to demonstrate what has been imagined or, yes, witnessed—in peace or, alas, here in war. The point, further, is for us to be shown something by certain boys and girls who become our teachers; thereby we are broadened and deepened responsively in our minds and hearts. ∎

INTRODUCTION
BY ANTHONY L. GEIST

They Still Draw Pictures: Children's Art in Wartime from the Spanish Civil War to Kosovo was published in conjunction with a traveling exhibition of the same title, sponsored by the Mandeville Special Collections Library at the University of California at San Diego and the Abraham Lincoln Brigade Archives. ALBA is both an archive in the traditional sense, housed at the Tamiment Library at New York University, and a living archive, devoted to preserving and spreading the legacy of the nearly 3000 young Americans who volunteered to defend Spanish democracy in the late 1930s. ALBA's Board of Governors, made up of Lincoln Brigade veterans, social activists, academics, writers, and artists, has sponsored numerous educational outreach activities, including the inspiration for this show, two remarkably successful traveling art exhibitions: "Shouts from the Wall: Posters and Photographs Brought Home from the Spanish Civil War by American Volunteers" and "Aura of the Cause: A Photo Album for North American Volunteers in the Spanish Civil War."

In the Spring of 1998 I was teaching a course on art and literature of the Spanish Civil War as a visiting professor at UCSD. I intended to put my students to work in the extraordinary Herbert Southworth Collection of materials from that war. As the director of Special Collections, Lynda Claassen, was giving me a tour of the holdings, she set before me a document case, which I opened to find over 600 drawings that had been created in refugee camps by Spanish children evacuated from war zones to the relative safety of the Mediterranean coast. I was stunned. The pictures spoke to me with a vibrancy and emotional power that spanned the more than sixty years that had lapsed since they were drawn. Lynda Claassen encouraged me to curate an exhibition and put the drawings at my disposal.

Subsequently, Peter N. Carroll, chair of the board of ALBA and co-curator of "They Still Draw Pictures," and I selected the Spanish drawings we found most expressive of the children's representation of their experiences of war. One of the things that most deeply moved us was our awareness that these little works of art constitute a contemporary as well as a historical problem, that children still suffer the savagery of war and still leave a record of their suffering in pictures. We selected a smaller number of children's drawings from later wars, from the Holocaust to Kosovo, that bear a tragic and uncanny resemblance to their Spanish counterparts.

The Spanish drawings trace a narrative line, from scenes of life before the war to war, evacuation, life in the refugee colonies, and visions of life after the war. Childen's art from more recent conflicts, drawn from many different sources and spanning the rest of the twentieth century, follows that narrative. By hanging these other drawings below the Spanish works they most closely parallel, we mean to suggest both the specificity of a particular historical circumstance and the universality of a child's response to the conditions of war and displacement.

The title of this book and the exhibition pays homage to the original collection of drawings (some of which are included here) that toured New York and Massachusetts in 1938. The catalog that accompanied that show, with an introduction by Aldous Huxley, went through three editions that year and the next.

"They Still Draw Pictures" is particularly significant to me, for it brings together my professional and personal life, my past and my present. I have studied and taught different aspects of the art and literature of the Spanish Civil War for most of my academic career. For the past twenty years I have worked closely with the Abraham Lincoln Brigade veterans.

As the son of parents who fought the good fight in the factories, shop floors, fields, and docks of California in the 1930s and '40s, I was raised on songs and stories of the labor movement and the Spanish Civil War. Lincoln vets Sidney Kaufmann and Luke Hinman were frequent guests at our table. Among my earliest visual images of Spain were the landscapes of Euskadi—filtered through memory and nostalgia—that our neighbor and friend Miguel Marina, exiled from the Spanish Basque country in 1939, spent the rest of his life painting.

As the father of young children whose own drawings are so similar to these—yet so profoundly different—my work on the exhibition seems to bridge the gap between the generations, between my daughters and the grandparents they never knew.

I have the sense of other circles closing too. It seems especially fitting that Sol R. Sender, grandson of the Spanish refugee novelist Ramón Sender, should have designed this beautiful book. Julián Zugazagoitia, whose grandfather, the eminent Spanish Socialist leader of the same name, was handed over to Franco by the Vichy government and executed in 1940, provided invaluable counsel and support as assistant to the director of the Guggenheim Museum in New York. Emilio Cassinello, consul general of Spain in New York, himself raised in exile in Mexico, encouraged this project from the start.

We have curated and organized "They Still Draw Pictures" to remind the world of this long-forgotten war, to chronicle the effects on its youngest victims, and to remember those who fought for their future. ■

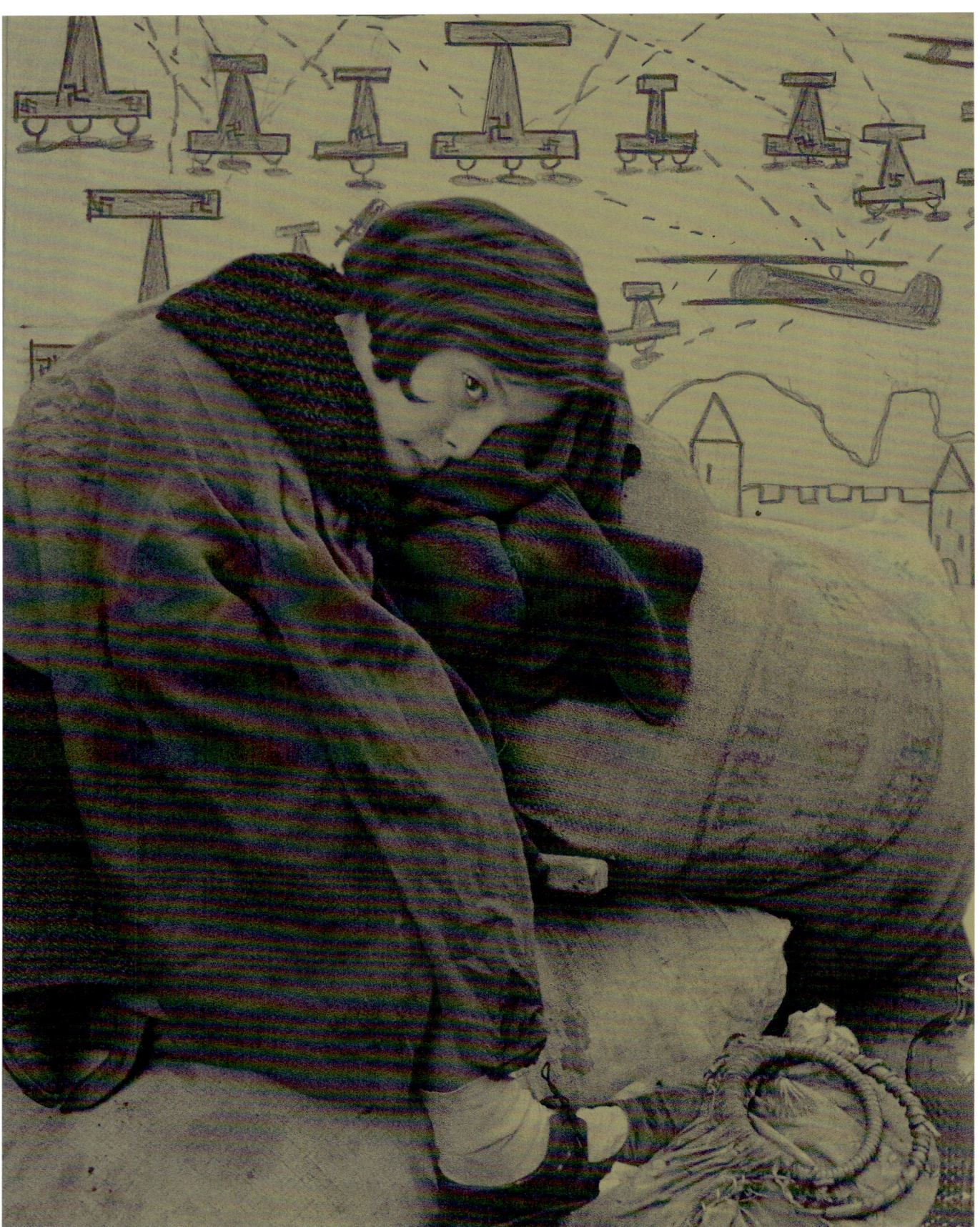

CHILDREN OF THE SPANISH CIVIL WAR

BY ANTHONY L. GEIST

14

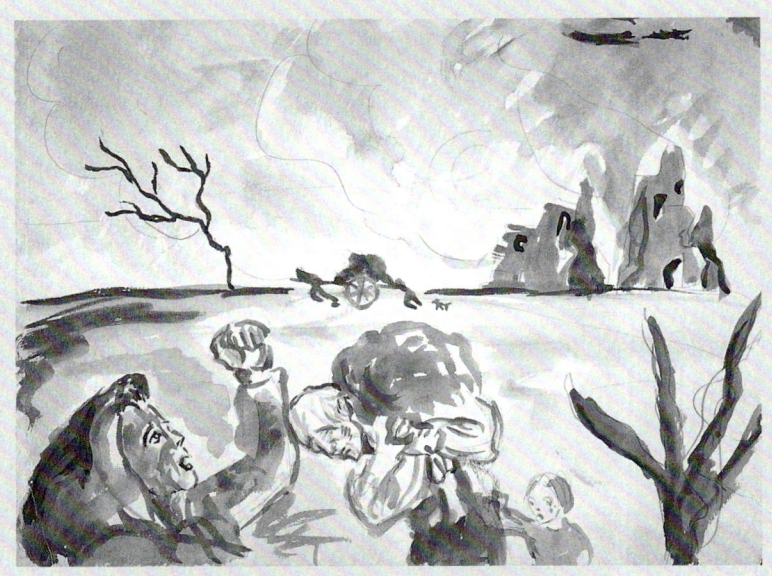

FIGURE 1
AUTHOR AND AGE UNKNOWN
WATERCOLOR FROM A REPUBLICAN REFUGEE CAMP, 1937–38
SEE PLATE 16

IN THE FOREGROUND, EYES RAISED IN ANGER AND IMPOTENCE, SHE SHAKES HER FIST AT THE THREE BOMBERS RECEDING INTO THE DISTANCE, LEAVING THE VILLAGE IN FLAMES. NEXT TO HER AND SLIGHTLY FARTHER FROM US, A CHILD CLUTCHES HER FATHER'S SHIRTTAILS AS HE SHOULDERS A BUNDLE, BENT UNDER THE WEIGHT OF A FEW POSSESSIONS SALVAGED FROM THE BOMBARDMENT....

15 CHILDREN OF THE SPANISH CIVIL WAR

In the middle distance, two men followed by a dog propel a loaded cart, leaning into the wind in a universal gesture of flight. Even the tree seems to tilt away from the scene of destruction. The power and pathos of this drawing are not to be found just in the woman's gesture of defiance and outrage or in the headlong career of the cart but precisely in the intersection of the diagonal axis of anger and the horizontal axis of flight. At one pole, the face of anguish; at the other, three anonymous black engines of death; at the point of their crossing, tiny figures fleeing in terror (fig. 1).

We know little about this watercolor. We do not know the author's name, only that she or he probably witnessed the scene depicted and was under sixteen years of age. We know that it was painted in a Republican refugee colony for children sometime in 1937 or 1938 and that it is now part of a collection of over 600 such drawings in the Southworth Collection at the University of California at San Diego's Mandeville Special Collections Library. Children's drawings from the Spanish Civil War (1936–39) have rarely been displayed in the United States since their first showing in New York and Massachusetts in 1938. Now a new traveling exhibition, "They Still Draw Pictures," once again brings these drawings to an American audience under the auspices of the Abraham Lincoln Brigade Archives and UCSD.

Women and children have been the victims of war since ancient times. In this bloodiest of centuries just drawn to a close, the wholesale slaughter of civilians has become tragically commonplace, from the unthinkable horrors of the Holocaust to recent revelations of U.S. atrocities in South Korea, from hundreds of My Lais in Southeast Asia to Rwanda, Bosnia, and Kosovo. Millions of women, children, and the aged were tortured, maimed, and murdered in what are now called "collateral damages." What, then, is so special about the Spanish Civil War? It was, after all, a relatively minor conflict waged over sixty years ago in a semi-modern nation on the fringes of Europe.

Spain was the first place to experience the horrors of modern mechanized warfare directed systematically against the civilian population. Franco's forces ringed Madrid from early in the war, confident that if the capital fell, so would the Republic. The government relocated to Valencia, yet the *madrileños* stubbornly defended their city. They stormed the military garrisons and armed themselves, built barricades with cobblestones, and rode trolley cars to the front in the University City and the Casa de Campo. Franco, backed by Nazi Germany and fascist Italy, responded by targeting for artillery and aerial bombardment working-class neighborhoods, hospitals, schools, the National Library, and the Prado Museum, hoping to break the backbone of the city's resistance. Madrid never fell; Colonel Casado finally surrendered it in March of 1939, and the war ended shortly thereafter.

Guernica, of course, is the most infamous example of what was at that time a new form of total warfare. A small town on Spain's northern coast—spiritual homeland to the Basque people—Guernica on April 26, 1937, suffered wave after wave of dive bombs, incendiary bombs, and strafing by the German Kondor Legion, testing its new warplanes and tactics in the service of Franco's forces. It was market day and people had come from surrounding towns and farms. The nearest military target, Bilbao, lay more than sixty kilometers away. The town was razed: 1,654 dead, 889 wounded (Thomas 419–423). Picasso immortalized Guernica in his enormous canvas of the same name, arguably his greatest painting and certainly his best known, which he created for the Spanish Pavilion at the 1937 Paris International Exhibition.

The representation of children's victimization in the art and literature of the Spanish Civil War is best understood in the context of the Republic's commitment to education, to culture, and to the children of Spain—that is, in its commitment to the future. When the Republic came to power in 1931 it inherited a country that had suffered for centuries under an absolute monarchy, allied with a repressive and powerful Catholic Church, a bloated landed aristocracy, and a top-heavy military at their service. I would like to quote from a thumbnail sketch of the country at that time. The statistics speak eloquently:

"Spain, 1931. 503,061 square kilometers, almost the size of France. Population 24 million, half of them—12 million—illiterate. 8 million living in poverty. 2 million landless peasants. 20,000 people own half of Spain. Entire provinces are the property of one family. The workers' average wage: between one and three pesetas per day. A kilo of bread costs one peseta. 20,000 monks, 31,000 priests, 60,000 nuns, 5,000 convents, 15,000 Army officers, 800 of them generals. One officer for every six men, one general for every 100 soldiers. A king, Alfonso XIII, the fourteenth sovereign since Isabel the Catholic Queen."

The Constitution of 1931 guaranteed freedom of worship and association, legalized civil marriage and divorce, and granted woman's suffrage. The new government initiated agrarian reform, reduced the power of the Church and the army, and undertook an ambitious educational project. Between 1931 and 1936 alone the Republic built thousands of new schools and trained teachers to staff them. These reforms threatened the wealth and power of the country's traditional

17

CHILDREN OF THE SPANISH CIVIL WAR

rulers and power-brokers. Their response was the military uprising of July 18, 1936, which became a bloody three-year war that in the end would cost nearly a million Spanish lives.

The Republic struggled to defend itself against its own army, bolstered by Germany and Italy. Denied foreign aid or access to international markets by Britain, France, and the United States, the embattled government nonetheless strove to wage war against fascism while maintaining its programs of social reform. The Republic continued to build schools throughout the war and initiated an ambitious adult literacy campaign through the Milicias de la Cultura (the Cultural Militia), who taught illiterate soldiers to read and write in the trenches.

The Republic's response to the refugee problem was another measure of its commitment to a culture based on humanist values. When the generals' failed coup turned into civil war, the country was bitterly divided. Some 600,000 refugees fled from Franco's tyranny into the relative security of Republican-controlled eastern Spain. Over 200,000 of them were children, many of them orphaned, others separated from their families or sent by their parents to safety. (Some estimates put the numbers much higher.) The government, short on food, medical supplies, and lodging, struggled to meet the needs of this massive influx of refugees. It understood that Spain's future lay with the children and turned its energies to them.

Faced with the problem of housing, clothing, feeding, and educating this vast number of displaced children, the government had two options: placing the young refugees with foster families, already strained by shortages, or creating group homes for them. The Republic's response—the establishment of *colonias infantiles* (children's colonies)—was at the cutting edge of a debate raging at that time in child welfare services throughout Europe and the United States. Virginia Malbin (fig. 2), one of a delegation of five young American women from the Social Workers Committee to Aid Spanish Democracy, spent several months in Spain in 1937 studying the *colonias infantiles* and designing a more efficient distribution of humanitarian aid from abroad. On her return to the States she wrote up her observations as a case study on group homes and published them as a two-part article in *Social Work Today*. She described the Spanish solution as the most progressive and humane response to the critical situation of caring for displaced children.

The French government offered refuge to 25,000 Basque children in camps in the south of France, while private relief agencies in

---

Cablegram from Mr. José A. Weissberger to the Spanish Child Welfare Association

Madrid
January 25, 1938

EVACUATION OF CHILDREN EXTREMELY SLOW AND DIFFICULT. (STOP) 134,000 CHILDREN STILL IN MADRID. (STOP) BEST ATTENTION GIVEN BY SELF-SACRIFICING STAFF OF DOCTORS AT DISPENSARIES. (STOP) TERRIFYING SHORTAGE COD LIVER OIL. (STOP) MILK SUPPLY RAPIDLY DWINDLING. (STOP) SUGAR SITUATION EVEN WORSE. (STOP) FORMERLY 75% MADRILENAS NURSED THEIR BABIES, NOW ONLY 10%. MOTHERS OFTEN FAINT OF WEAKNESS AT DISPENSARIES WITH BABIES IN THEIR ARMS. (STOP) TUBERCULOSIS RAPIDLY INCREASING. (STOP) LACK OF SOAP CAUSING SERIOUS SKIN DISEASES. (STOP) MOST CHILDREN OVER TWELVE LAST YEAR NEITHER GREW NOR GAINED WEIGHT, MOTHERS GIVING PREFERENCE TO YOUNGEST. (STOP). SITUATION IN PROVINCES SLIGHTLY BETTER IN ORANGE GROWING DISTRICTS. (STOP) QUAKER MILK DISPENSARIES BARCELONA DOING SPLENDID WORK. SAME BADLY NEEDED IN MADRID. (STOP) TRANSPORT PROBLEM DIFFICULT. ASSOCIATION SHOULD HAVE SEVERAL MOTOR LORRIES. (STOP) GOING TO VALENCIA ON SATURDAY.

WEISSBERGER

José A. Weissberger, a former prominent businessman from Madrid, worked closely with the New York–based Spanish Child Welfare Association, which published *They Still Draw Pictures* (1938), with a foreword by Aldous Huxley. Weissberger edited the volume.

England took in another 4000, the Soviet Union 2000, and Mexico 500. The Republican government, however, through its Secretariat for Evacuation and Assistance of Refugees and the Ministry of Health and Education, cared for the bulk of the children (Collins 8). Other centers were established and operated by international non-governmental agencies, such as the Red Cross and International Red Aid, as well as various units of the International Brigades, as can be seen in the names of organizations stamped on many of the drawings. Whenever possible the Republic set up *colonias infantiles*, often in requisitioned country estates and mansions abandoned by fascist sympathizers, along the coast or in the mountains. The colonies had resident teachers and medical personnel to attend to the educational, physical, emotional, and psychological needs of the children.

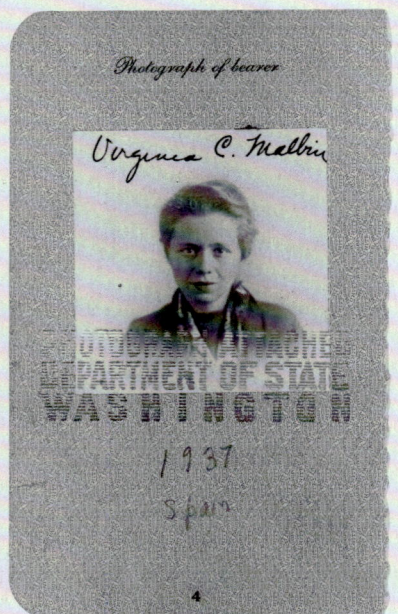

FIGURE 2
VIRGINIA MALBIN'S PASSPORT PHOTOGRAPH

Despite the government's efforts, there were never enough colonies to accommodate all the child refugees, as we see in the testimony offered by Alfonso Ortuño, whose living conditions with a foster family were at times difficult ("Interview").

The civil war was remarkable for a number of reasons. The Republic's commitment to education, culture, and the welfare of children found its corollary in the outpouring of support and sympathy worldwide for the Spanish people's defense of democracy. With the rise of fascism in Europe, with Hitler in power in Germany and Mussolini's invasion of Ethiopia, Spain was perceived as the first place to fight back. Some 40,000 volunteers from over fifty countries joined the International Brigades to defend the Republic in an unprecedented show of international solidarity.

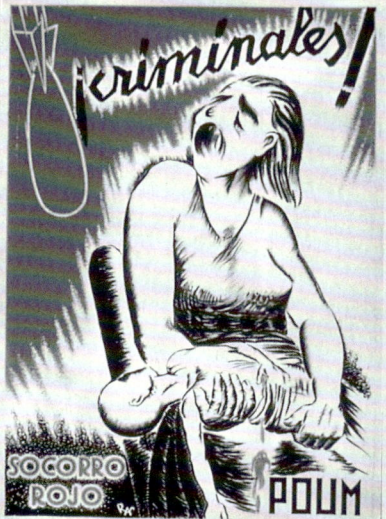

FIGURE 3
POSTER ISSUED BY POUM RED AID

Artists, intellectuals, and writers in overwhelming numbers, in Spain and throughout the world, forsook the avant-garde aesthetic of the 1920s and put their art at the service of the Spanish Republic. The plight of children was a common theme in the iconography and literature of the war. The vulnerability of children and the violation of their trust and innocence provided powerful images of protest. Of the more than 1800 posters produced on the Loyalist side during the war, for instance, a significant number featured children as innocent victims. Called "Shouts from the Wall" (*gritos pegados a la pared*), Republican poster art, designed, let's remember, for a largely illiterate population, communicated through strong graphic images. The poster issued by POUM Red Aid (whose militia George Orwell joined in 1937) could not be more powerful in its eloquent simplicity (fig. 3). Against a red backdrop a woman sketched in black and white cradles a dead baby in her arms. Counterpoised to the bomb falling behind her, she raises her head in anguish to the sky, mouth open in a silent scream reminiscent of Kathe Kolwitz's powerful canvases. The diagonal red and black composition suggests the Anarchist colors. "¡Criminales!" (criminals, murderers) is the only verbal message, its letters parallel to the inert body of the child, tracing an implicit link between the two. Cary Nelson speculates that this poster may have influenced Picasso's *Guernica* (Nelson 1996).

Another style of poster, this one issued in various languages by the Madrid Defense Council, uses a photomontage technique pioneered a few years earlier in Germany by John Heartfield (fig. 4). The almost unbearable image of a dead child, a victim of terror bombardment, lies before us in the starkest documentary realism. The numbers around her neck suggest a morgue photo; mouth and eyes gaping, she is frozen in the immediacy of death. Behind her fly in perfect geometrical formation the planes responsible for this carnage. The fragility of the flesh—the dead girl in close-up and yet irretrievably distant in the solitude of death—superimposed on the depersonalized engines of mechanized destruction speak powerfully to our sensibilities. Cary Nelson reminds us that most residents of Madrid or Barcelona during the war would have seen dead children after any bombing raid and that their aestheticization through the modernist technique of photomontage allowed for a process of abstraction, enabling them to move from purely personal empathy to ideological and political mobilization (Nelson 1996, 24).

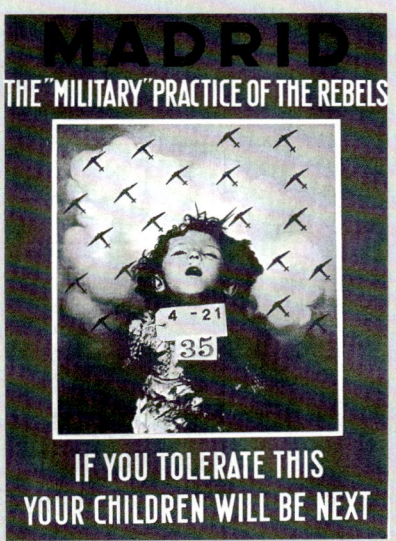

FIGURE 4
POSTER ISSUED BY MADRID DEFENSE COUNCIL

Poets, too, seized on the image of the child as innocent victim. The Chilean poet Pablo Neruda, later Nobel Laureate, had been posted to Spain as a cultural attaché during the early years of the Republic and formed close friendships with his Spanish contemporaries: Federico García Lorca, Rafael Alberti, and Miguel Hernández among them. He remained in Madrid for a significant period during the war and wrote one of the most compelling books of poetry to come out of the conflict. In "I Explain a Few Things," one of the most anthologized of the poems that make up *Spain in the Heart* (1938), he simultaneously addresses aesthetic and political issues.

YOU WILL ASK: AND WHERE ARE THE LILIES?
AND THE METAPHYSICAL BLANKET OF POPPIES?
AND THE RAIN THAT OFTEN BEAT ON
HIS WORDS, FILLING THEM
WITH HOLES AND BIRDS?

LET ME TELL YOU EVERYTHING THAT'S GOING ON WITH ME.

Neruda's rhetorical questions that open the poem refer to a change in poetics that he and his entire generation throughout Europe and the Americas experienced in the 1930s, the move from an avant-garde, post-romantic ideal of art for art's sake to an aesthetics of social and political commitment. Neruda answers his questions first by describing the beauty and vitality of pre-war Madrid—the flowered terraces, bustling streets, and bountiful markets of his neighborhood—and then their destruction.

AND ONE MORNING IT WAS ALL IN FLAMES,
ONE MORNING BLAZING FIRES,
CAME OUT OF THE EARTH,
DEVOURING PEOPLE,
AND SINCE THEN, FIRE,
GUNPOWDER SINCE THEN,
AND SINCE THEN, BLOOD.

Neruda centers the devastation on the figure of the child:

OUTLAWS WITH PLANES AND MOORS,
OUTLAWS WITH JEWELS AND DUCHESSES,
OUTLAWS WITH BLACK FRIARS OFFERING THEIR BLESSING,
CAME THROUGH THE SKIES TO KILL CHILDREN,
AND IN THE STREETS THE BLOOD OF CHILDREN,
RAN SIMPLY, LIKE CHILDREN'S BLOOD.

He follows with a metaphorical description of the effects of the fascist savagery: rather than defeat, greater resistance. He uses a figure common to other poets of the war as well: death sows the seed of renewed struggle.

BUT FROM EACH DEAD CHILD COMES A RIFLE WITH EYES,
BUT FROM EACH MURDER ARE BORN BULLETS
THAT ONE DAY WILL FIND THEIR WAY
TO YOUR HEARTS.

The next-to-last stanza reiterates the questions that opened the poem:

YOU WILL ASK: WHY DOES HIS POETRY
NOT SPEAK TO US OF DREAMS, OF THE LEAVES,
OF THE GREAT VOLCANOES OF HIS NATIVE COUNTRY?

Life and death, he answers, make such poetry impossible now.

(VENID A VER LA SANGRE POR LAS CALLES,	COME SEE THE BLOOD IN THE STREETS,
VENID A VER	COME SEE
LA SANGRE POR LAS CALLES,	THE BLOOD IN THE STREETS,
VENID A VER LA SANGRE	COME SEE THE BLOOD
POR LAS CALLES)	IN THE STREETS!

21 CHILDREN OF THE SPANISH CIVIL WAR

Another great Latin American poet, the Peruvian César Vallejo, was fiercely committed to the cause of the Spanish Republic. When he died in poverty in Paris a year after attending the Congress of Anti-Fascist Writers in 1937 in Valencia and Madrid, his dying words were "Spain, I'm going to Spain." In his magnificent *Spain, Take This Cup from Me* (1938), Vallejo approaches both poetry and the image of the child differently from Neruda. He is one of the few poets of the war to express socially committed themes in thoroughly avant-garde verse, for he believed that the poetic revolution was inseparable from social revolution. Hence his language is often more cryptic, his images denser, than those of his contemporaries, but no less effective for it. (Indeed, some would argue precisely the opposite.)

In poem XIV, which gives its title to the book, Vallejo calls upon the "children of the world" to save "mother teacher Spain." He links their fate to hers: should she fall, they will never develop and forever be locked in ignorance. Vallejo, in his lifelong obsession with the written word, represents the plight of children should Spain fall in terms of writing and language: "diphthong," "downstroke," "inkwell," "alphabet," even "teeth," which articulate and pronounce the word.

(SI CAE ESPAÑA—DIGO, ES UN DECIR—)

IF SPAIN FALLS—I MEAN, IT'S JUST A THOUGHT—IF SPAIN
FALLS, FROM THE EARTH DOWNWARD,
CHILDREN, HOW YOU WILL STOP GROWING!
HOW THE YEAR WILL PUNISH THE MONTH!
HOW YOU WILL NEVER HAVE MORE THAN TEN TEETH,
HOW THE DIPHTHONG WILL NEVER BE MORE THAN
DOWNSTROKE, THE MEDAL NO MORE THAN TEARS!
HOW THE LITTLE LAMB WILL CONTINUE
TIED BY ITS LEG TO THE GREAT INKWELL!
HOW YOU WILL DESCEND THE STEPS OF THE ALPHABET
TO THE LETTER IN WHICH PAIN WAS BORN!

Vallejo's depiction of the children's suffering should fascism prevail, however, does not stop at their victimization. Neruda imagined that rifles would spring from the graves of children. Vallejo exhorts the children of the world to defend Spain:

LOWER YOUR BREATHING, AND IF
HER FOREARM DROPS,
IF THE SPLINT RESOUNDS, IF IT IS NIGHT,
IF HEAVEN FITS IN TWO TERRESTRIAL LIMBOS,
IF THERE'S NOISE IN THE SOUND OF THE DOORS,
IF I AM LATE,
IF YOU DON'T SEE ANYONE, IF THE UNSHARPENED PENCILS
FRIGHTEN YOU, IF MOTHER
SPAIN FALLS—I MEAN, IT'S JUST A THOUGHT—

(SALID, NIÑOS DEL MUNDO; ID A BUSCARLA!...) GO, CHILDREN OF THE WORLD, GO LOOK FOR HER!...

The Hungarian Robert Capa, whose photographs from the Spanish Civil War would define photojournalism for the rest of the century, also portrayed the effects of the war on children. His most moving images do not capture the death and maiming of young victims as much as the solitude of their suffering. This picture, one of a series taken of Republicans about to leave Barcelona for exile in France in 1939, at the very end of the war, captures the particular pathos of displacement (fig. 5). The girl, wrapped in an adult's coat, lies on the crudely packed bundles of her family's possessions. She stares somewhere off camera. Her posture—feet tucked up, hands clasping her knees, out of sight under the coat, her absent gaze, the collar pulled up around her neck—all suggest that she has drawn deep within herself. One would never guess that she is surrounded by perhaps 150 other people in motion, talking, moving bundles, preparing to leave, which Capa caught in earlier shots in the sequence. At the moment of the photograph she is radically alone.

In the next photo, which Capa took on the road from Barcelona to the French border in 1939, the boy is in motion but travels alone (fig. 6). He traverses an archetypal Spanish landscape: flat, windswept, nearly bare of vegetation. The few scrubby bushes rising behind him to the right merely accentuate the absence of others. The rough, wool army blanket slung crosswise over his shoulders, an icon of the Republican militias, stands in contrast to his short pants, the emblem of his youth. His bare legs express vulnerability. Capa's photo gives us little context: Where is his family? Where is he coming from? Where is he going? We have no answers, just the image of a solitary figure moving though an enormous empty space.

The Republic established the children's colonies precisely to combat the intense isolation visited upon children in times of war. One of the most remarkable things to emerge from these remarkable institutions were thousands of drawings done by the children, such as those in the Southworth Collection. A typewritten dispatch bearing the stamp of the Spanish Information Bureau and signed by Kate Mangan gives a contemporary account of the children's drawings. Mangan reports that 3000 drawings were first displayed in Valencia in May 1937 in an exhibition organized by the Provincial Committee of the Ministry of Education. Of them, 118 were selected for showing in England and the United States to raise funds for children's relief efforts in Spain. The American Friends Service Committee and the Carnegie Institute in Madrid also participated in the collection and exhibition of the children's artwork. Aldous Huxley wrote an introduction to the exhibit catalog, which went through three printings in 1938 and 1939.

23 CHILDREN OF THE SPANISH CIVIL WAR

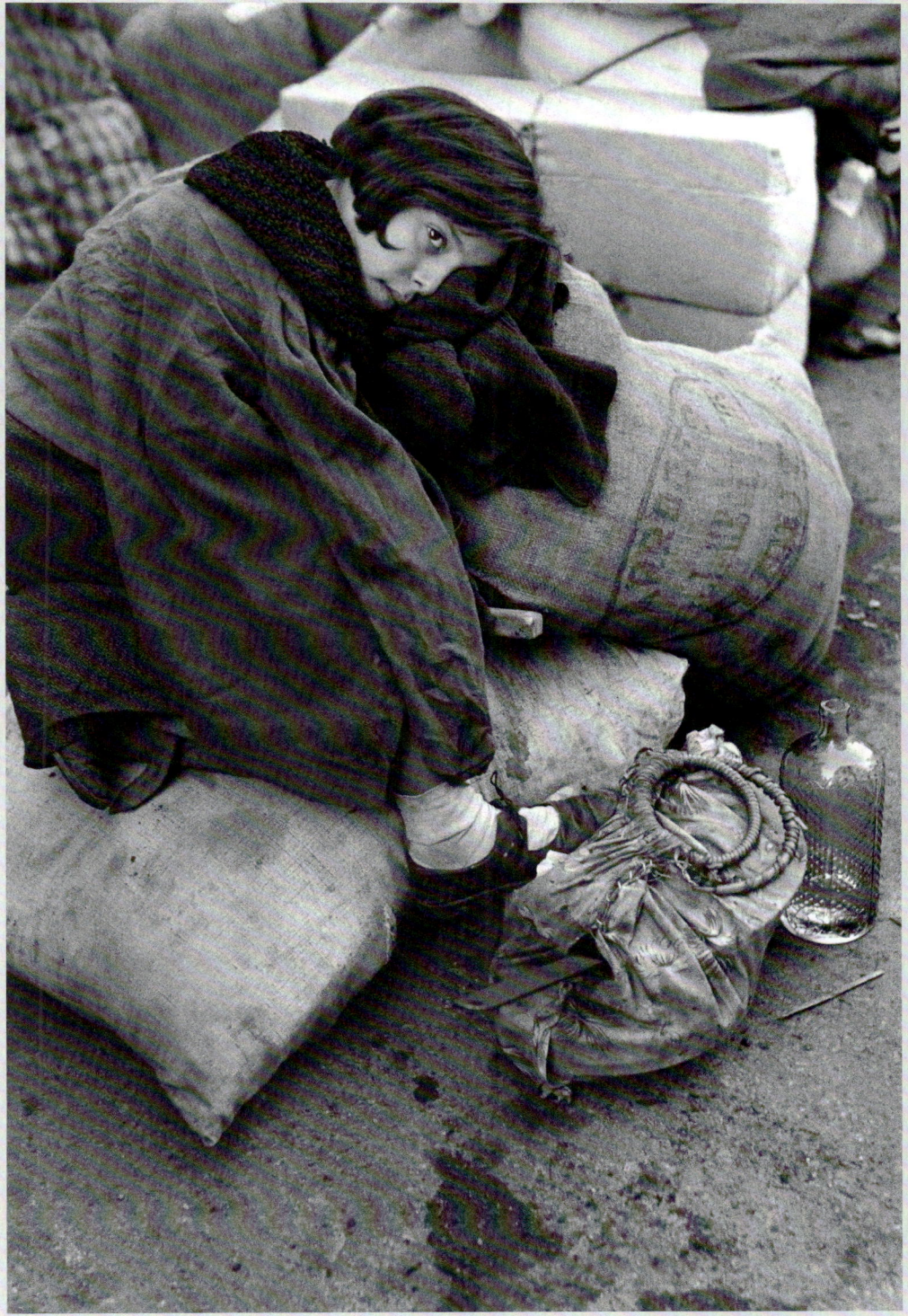

FIGURE 5
PHOTOGRAPH BY ROBERT CAPA
BARCELONA, JANUARY 1939

COURTESY OF CORNELL CAPA

"IT IS NOT ALWAYS EASY TO STAND ASIDE AND BE UNABLE TO DO ANYTHING EXCEPT RECORD THE SUFFERINGS AROUND ONE."
— ROBERT CAPA

The images and texts produced by adult artists that I have just discussed are without question powerful, moving, and effective, yet the children's drawings affect us differently. The posters, Neruda, Vallejo, and Capa represent the suffering of children under conditions of war. They are designed to evoke sympathy and outrage in other adults. In the drawings from the colonies the children depict their own experiences. Their self-representation gives them a subjectivity and agency as historical subjects that they cannot achieve as objects of adult artists. The drawings offer us a view of children as participants in the historical drama of the civil war. Nearly all the pictures are signed and the young artists are identified by their age and the location of the colony. Until recently we knew nothing about them: what became of them after the war, whether they are still living, and where they live. With the assistance of the Spanish consul general in New York and the Ministry of the Interior, I have now located twelve surviving authors of the drawings in the UCSD collection. An interview with one of them appears in this book.

For these reasons the drawings are especially valuable as a collective testimony of children's experiences of the war. Nicholas Stargardt, writing about drawings from the Terezin concentration camp in Czechoslovakia, reminds us, "We need to think about subjectivity in a synchronic and collective sense, rather than in the diachronic terms of individual biography—as the frozen moments of a social history lived in a very particular time and location" (16). Through the graphic testimony of the drawings we can reconstruct the physical and emotional effects wrought on thousands of young Spaniards by the trauma of the war.

The drawings from the *colonias infantiles* in Spain represent perhaps the earliest evidence of organized art therapy. Anna Freud and Melanie Klein's debate over the development of the child's ego and affective attachment disorders was based to a great extent on the former's studies of the drawings made by refugee children from London, who were evacuated to orphanages and institutions in the English countryside. There they were beyond the reach of German bombs and V-2 rockets but also beyond loving human touch. Such apparently was not the case of the Spanish children's colonies.

On examining the drawings from the *colonias* one is struck, as with all children's art, by their immediacy and spontaneity. They have a kind of Benjaminian "aura" of authenticity in the untutored representation of the child's world. They possess an innocence—perhaps the innocence of untrained technique—even as they represent unspeakable horrors. Picasso said, "Once I drew like Rafael, but it has taken me a lifetime to draw like a child" (in Collins 18). That childlike or childish quality is precisely what gives these drawings their special emotional power.

Teachers in the colonies assigned set topics, and the children responded enthusiastically. Virginia Malbin recalls that in one group home she visited they had to limit to two the number of drawings the residents were allowed to submit to the house newsletter (interview, August 1998). For the purposes of this book I have organized the drawings into five categories: Memories of Loss (Before the War), War, Evacuation and Displacement, Colonies and Camps, and Visions of Peace (After the War). I will take them up in that order.

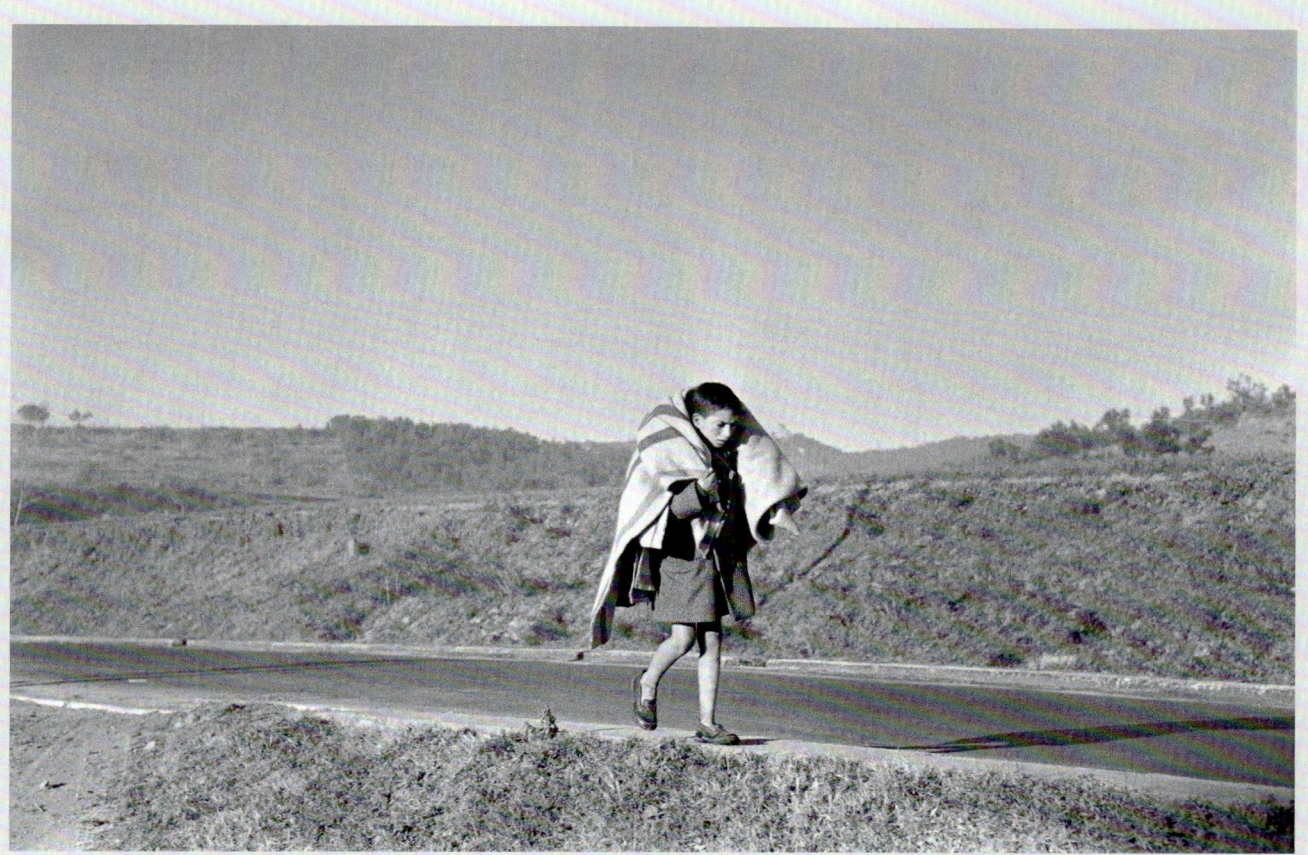

FIGURE 6
PHOTOGRAPH BY ROBERT CAPA
ON THE ROAD FROM BARCELONA TO THE FRENCH BORDER
JANUARY 25–27, 1939

COURTESY OF CORNELL CAPA

26

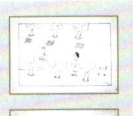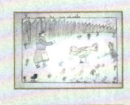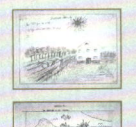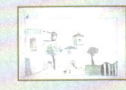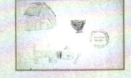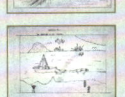

SEE COLOR PLATES PAGES 54–57

BEFORE
ANTES **VORHER** AVANT **PRIMA**

MEMORIES OF LOSS

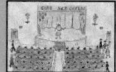
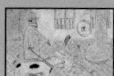

27

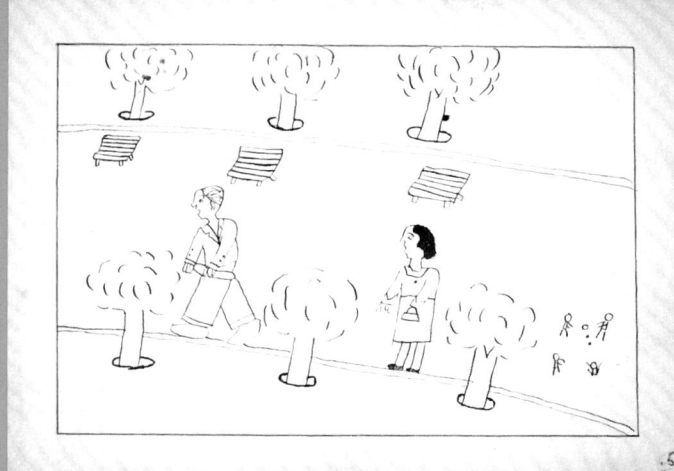

FIGURE 7
CARMEN SIERRA
AGE 12
SEE PLATE 1

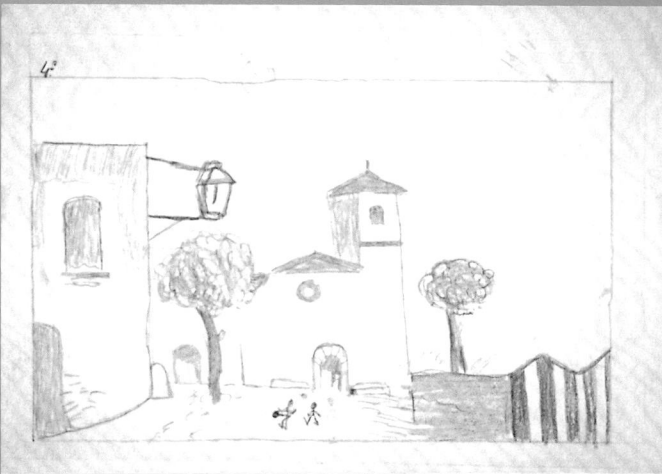

FIGURE 8
LUIS VERGARA
AGE 11
SEE PLATE 2

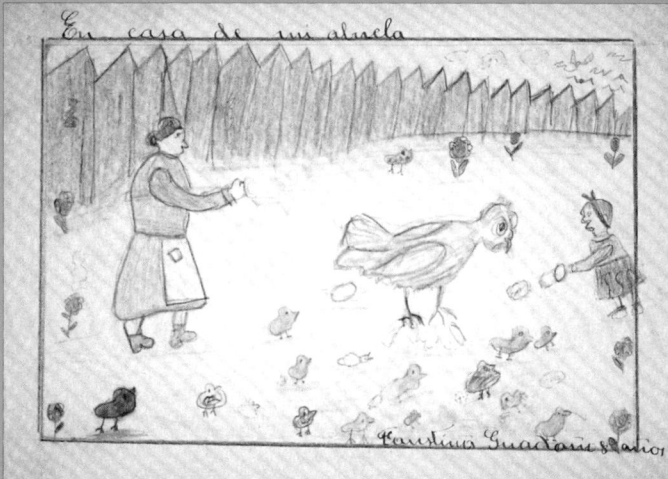

FIGURE 9
FAUSTINA GUADAÑO
AGE 8
SEE PLATE 3

ANTES

Among the most moving of the drawings are those that depict images of peace, either of life before the war or visions of the future. The drawings in the first grouping—life before the war—vary considerably in topic and execution, but all have an orderly air about them, a sense of the quotidian, of daily life as usual. They depict ordinary people—often featuring the artist as protagonist—doing ordinary things: a stroll in the park, returning from school, washing clothes, feeding the chickens. As we will also see in the representations of life in the colonies, the children render these scenes in loving detail. They evoke and idealize home, preserving on paper what they may never see again. Nicholas Stargardt, talking about drawings from the Holocaust, remarks on the "careful guarding of memory" of life before the war as a way of salvaging the past, uncertain if they will ever be able to recover it.

Carmen Sierra (age 12) draws an urban park scene (fig. 7 or plate 1). Well-tended trees flank the path in two orderly rows. Carefully drafted park benches await passersby. A man and a woman walk from right to left. He holds what appears to be a loaf of bread in his left hand; she, a purse. They are talking, perhaps arguing. In the lower right-hand corner four tiny children play catch. Their rendering as stick figures without facial features stands in contrast to the adults, represented in realistic detail—cuffs and buttons, hair and faces, shoes and purse meticulously drawn. These are the stable features of the child's world; they are what matter and merit attention.

Luis Vergara's vision of a village plaza emphasizes the importance of place (fig. 8 or plate 2). The eleven-year-old renders the square, church rising in the back, the street lamp hanging over the scene, as solid and intact, as it will always remain in his memory. As in so many of the drawings the disproportionately small human figures are relatively unimportant and impersonal. What matters is the permanence of place.

Faustina Guadaño remembers her grandmother's house from afar (fig. 9 or plate 3). She feeds a hen larger than herself as its chicks scurry around them. The disproportion, the error of realistic representation, reveals an emotional truth far greater than accuracy of scale could.

The teachers also assigned free drawing (*dibujo libre*). Nearly all those marked as such depict a peaceable kingdom, the sun smiling on a brightly colored world. I am particularly attracted to Esperanza Sanz's drawing of a dog with a bone. In its Miró-like naiveté it evokes the essence of domesticity (fig. 10 or plate 4). The sun also presides over Alejandro Chilián's view of peacetime: house drawn in perfect symmetry, the orderly orchard framing the ploughman's straight furrows (fig. 11 or plate 5).

It is often difficult to determine whether the free drawings represent life before or after the war. I think we must understand them simply as life without war. In either case, this is the world the child refugees only have access to in memory or imagination, images of peace fixed in color and shapes on paper. ∎

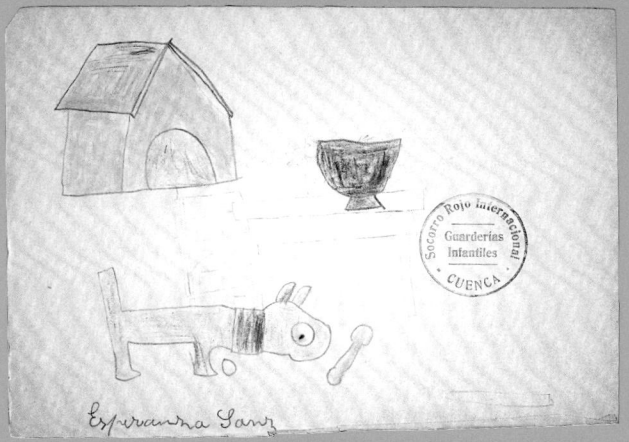

FIGURE 10
ESPERANZA SANZ
AGE UNKNOWN
SEE PLATE 4

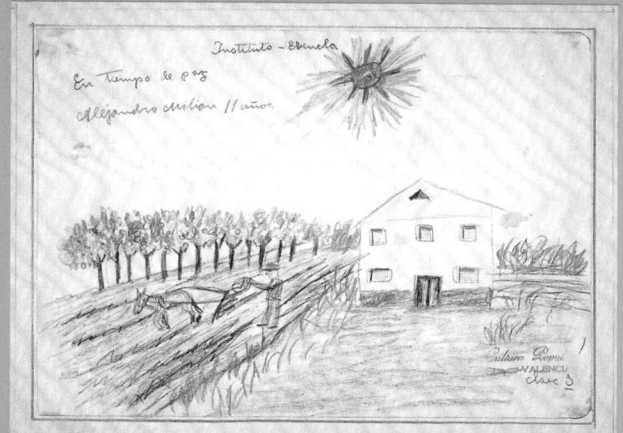

FIGURE 11
ALEJANDRO CHILIÁN
AGE 11
SEE PLATE 5

30

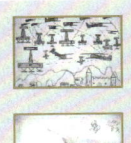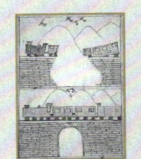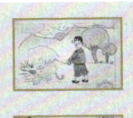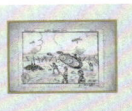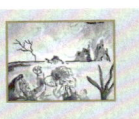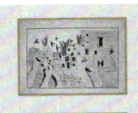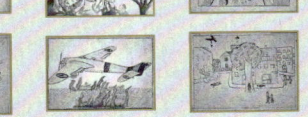

SEE COLOR PLATES PAGES 58-67

WAR
GUERRA **LUFTË** KRIEG **GUERRE**

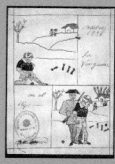 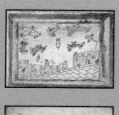 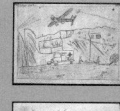 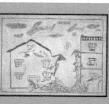
 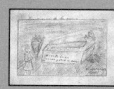 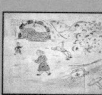

"THE DANGEROUS THING IS TO HAVE EYES":
LETTER FROM MARTHA GELLHORN TO ELEANOR ROOSEVELT

Dearest Mrs. Roosevelt,

    I got back from Barcelona this morning and found your letter. The report about the refugees in Czechoslovakia was full of terrible things, and I could write you a long letter about the food situation in Spain, with special reference to children, that is quite as tragic. But I won't. Not now. You and the President are much loved in that country. About 60,000 children are eating a half a pound of whole wheat bread, each day, for this month: so when I wander around schools seeing them they say to me (any American is a representative of yours in their eyes) "Many thanks, and many greetings for the President and the Señora Roosevelt."

    They also draw pictures, because with some food in them (that's all the food they have in them) they feel very lively and happy: so they make wonderful pictures of the Quakers—who distribute this food—in their home, which is called the White House, and the pictures are signed: Para el Presidente Roosevelt, Juanito Menendez, 10 años. There is some confusion as to who is God, whether it is the Quakers, or the Red Cross, or the White House, or the Roosevelts. But all they know is that God sends them bread. The children eating these huge hunks of dry bread was about the only happy thing I saw. I was in various schools during air raids and the children waited patiently and sadly for it to finish, because until the raids finished they would not get their bread. So it goes. I cannot yet understand why there must be so much suffering. I shall never be a good writer, the human animal escapes me. Because evidently, the men in the planes have families too, and the men who sink the food ships have families, and the men who run a war have sons who can also get killed, but none of this seems to have any serious effect upon behavior.

    I shall be home December 20 and very glad of it. I am tired in the head. There is no escape from the world and how it runs, at least I don't know of any escape but maybe the Atlantic serves as a buffer and one will not see so much or feel so guilty about it. The dangerous thing is to have eyes. Nowadays, with a pair of eyes you can be pretty sure you will not have much rest or peace. War itself, war in the trenches between armed men, is of course bad enough, but it is a circus compared to the helpless Jews living in ditches between Czecho and Germany, and the helpless solitary man caught up in the ghastly machinery of the concentration camp, and the seven months old babies with rickets or t.b. in Barcelona. I do not think danger is terrible and I am not sure I think sudden death is terrible—at least if you are fighting against something that makes living valueless—but lonely persecution and starvation and the fear of the women alone in their flimsy houses with the children, when the night bombers come over: well, those things are too bad. And so I was not going to write you a grim letter, and enough of it.

    If you have time to see me, I would love it, and perhaps you could send me a note to my brother's house at 44 Riverside Drive, if you did have time. By the way, I saw the Goya etchings Luis Quintanilla is bringing over to you and what wonders they are. It is a genuine emotion and not a formal state gesture to give those pictures to you. And now in Europe, all the time, one is very proud to be American. I do hope I can see you. My plans are vague. What I hope for more than anything is to go back to Connecticut for six months and do a book. It would be wonderful to write again and to sit still, wonderful and fairly necessary. What do you suppose historians will make of this decade, one hundred years from now. I doubt if they will be able to reconstruct it or believe in it, it is too fantastic, and it goes too fast, but I should think the Dark Ages will seem neon-lighted in comparison.

    I do look forward to seeing you, if you are not too busy.

                                    Always devotedly,

                                    [signed] Marty

Paris
December 3 [1938]

GEIST

Among the most numerous and powerful drawings in the Southworth Collection are those depicting war. They are also the most numerous in this book. Here I will comment on several of the most representative and significant. They vary greatly in style and skill of execution; they depict cityscapes and country scenes, yet almost all of them have one thing in common: airplanes. Aerial combat and bombing were new, and the greatest terror came from the air. The children drew the planes in remarkably accurate detail. Aviation historians can identify most of the models in the drawings: Henkels trimotors, Messerschmidts, Russian "chatos," and so forth.

"They move like mechanized doom," Robert Jordan remarks of the airplanes in Hemingway's *For Whom the Bell Tolls* (87). One Spanish child, Rafael Morante, was five years old in 1936, vacationing with his family in Almería when Nazi warships shelled the Mediterranean resort. He recalls a feeling of dread as he ran up the coast road, clutching his mother's hand, as shells exploded around them:

"I THOUGHT THE WORLD HAD COME TO AN END, AND WOULD NEVER BE THE SAME AGAIN..."

(Interview, Havana, Cuba, July 20, 2000).

GUERRA

Rafael Barber, ten years old, drew this picture in the Colonia Escolar Colectiva de Burriana, in the eastern province of Castellón (fig. 12 or plate 9). Nazi warplanes fill the sky from edge to edge of the neatly traced border that frames the drawing, as though hoping to contain the violence. Their murderous geometry occupies nearly the entire composition. The strict linearity of the airplanes, reminiscent of an Italian futurist painting, contrasts with the asymmetrical landscape below. If we understand the buildings to be drafted on a human scale, we realize that the bombers and fighters dwarf them. Their larger than life size, though compositionally incorrect, rings true emotionally. The castle, a remnant of medieval warfare, is useless to protect the village against the blitzkrieg. The absence of any sign of human life increases the pathos of this piece.

The next drawing, whose author is unidentified other than by the initials E.G. etched on the keystone of the bridge in the bottom panel, is unusual for its narrative structure (fig. 13 or plate 11). It presents a before and after that must be read from bottom to top. The lower panel shows a train crossing a bridge; the sun (curiously frowning) peeks between two mountains. The nearly perfect bilateral symmetry, centered on the vertical axis of the sun and the tunnel under the bridge, suggests peace and order. In the upper panel, the planes retreat after having destroyed the bridge and the train, upsetting the order and symmetry of the "before." Even one of the mountains has disappeared. The anonymous child artist seems to have intuited in his or her elliptical narrative what Madison Avenue advertising agencies learned much later: that stories can be told with just the beginning and the end.

Miguel Ercaño García's drawing shows remarkable sophistication for a twelve-year-old (fig. 14 or plate 10). It holds a power, horror, and nobility evocative of Goya's *Disasters of War*. The picture has no true center; its simple narrative develops from right to left. In the background, distance indicated by size rather than perspective, a soldier whips a man lashed to a tree. In the middle

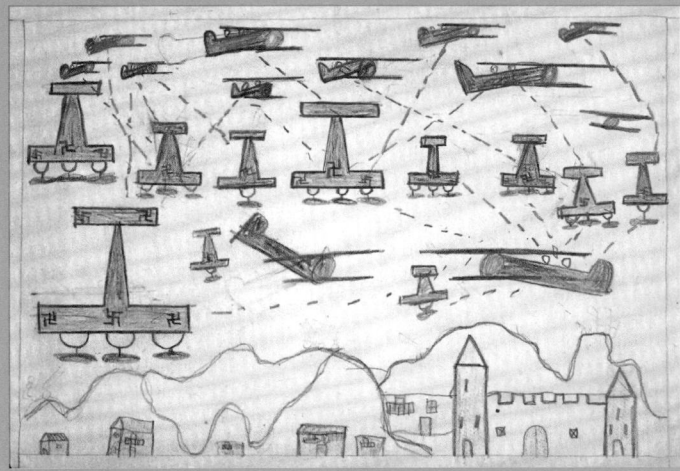

FIGURE 12
RAFAEL BARBER
AGE 10
SEE PLATE 9

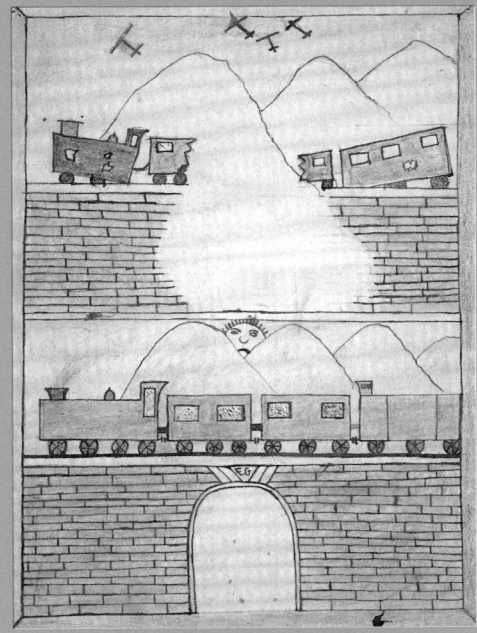

FIGURE 13
E.G.
AGE UNKNOWN
SEE PLATE 11

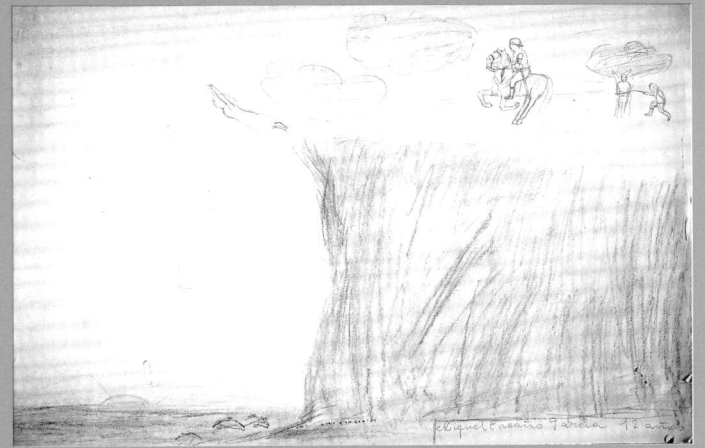

FIGURE 14
MIGUEL ERCAÑO GARCÍA
AGE 12
SEE PLATE 10

34 GUERRA

ground another soldier on horseback pursues a woman, who leaps off a cliff to escape him. The rocky shore awaits her below. The sun, we have no way of knowing whether rising or setting, hangs at the exact diagonal opposite the whipping. While the young artist has sketched the defining gesture of the picture—the woman's plunge to the sea—with simple lines, he has rendered the horseman in minute detail: the horse's trappings accurate, the rider's uniform a perfect reproduction of that worn by the Spanish cavalry, from the Nazi-style helmet down to the sword and boots. A swastika adorns his armband. Evil, the detail implies, must be studied closely. Yet the woman reappears as a ghostly palimpsest over the sea. The serenity of her face, full front and in profile, lends an air of hope to this otherwise bleak scene.

The child artists of the *colonias infantiles* depict war in many different ways, but one rarely finds expressions of pure fantasy among them. That makes this drawing, by the twelve-year-old Margarita Arnao Crespo, so unique (fig. 15 or plate 12). It shares many of the characteristics common to children's art across nations and cultures: in the background are trees, clouds, and mountains, the sun peeking through them; in the foreground, a central figure. Yet this is not a scene witnessed or remembered. Rendered in cheerful colors, it is a fanciful allegory of the triumph over fascism. A boy, a smile creasing his face, swings his ax at a fantastic fascist beast. Significantly, it is a child (we know by his short pants and shoes) who drives the beast from the land. Equally significantly, the artist, a girl, depicts not herself but a boy as hero.

Numerous other representations of war show a great variety of styles and skill of execution. Notice particularly the naval battle (plate 13), tank warfare (plate 14), and hand-to-hand combat (plate 15). ■

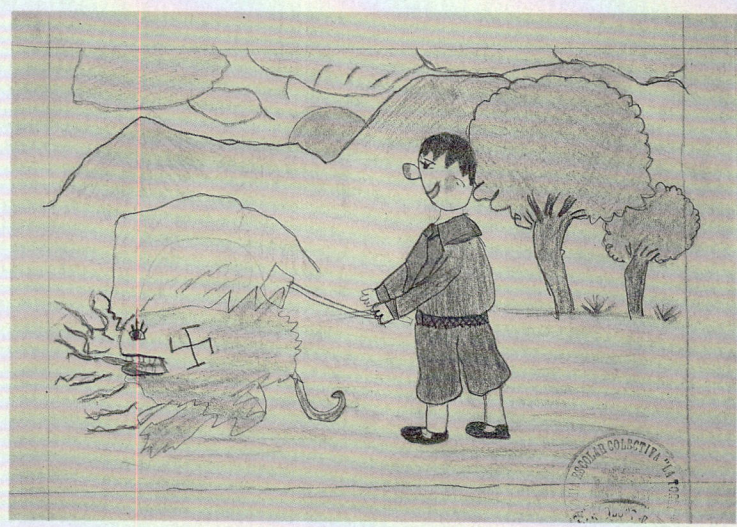

FIGURE 15
MARGARITA ARNAO CRESPO
AGE 12
SEE PLATE 12

35

CHILDREN OF KOSOVO 1999

This drawing was created in the summer of 1999 by a sixteen-year-old Kosovar girl in a refugee camp in Albania, operated by the United Nations High Commissioner for Refugees. The artist's name has been withheld for reasons of security. Volunteers from the United States, Western Europe, and Asia worked with the children in art therapy projects to express their experiences of war and to begin a process of healing.

Coming at the end of the twentieth century, this sketch bears a tragic and uncanny resemblance to many of the Spanish drawings. Sixty years later aviation still occupies a privileged position. While the teenage artist has perfected perspective (witness the rendering of the house in flames), the NATO fighter is unnaturally large, emphasizing its importance. It dwarfs the clearly identified Serbian tank and its target, the burning dwelling.

All three objects are drawn in extremely simple lines. In fact, they could scarcely be represented more schematically: the house, a cube; the flames consuming it, red and orange scribbles; the tank, a combination of rectangles and circles; even the fighter plane is drawn in the simplest of strokes. As such, they stand as icons of war in the young refugee's depiction.

While the NATO bombing campaign against Milosevic's forces polarized world opinion, this drawing leaves little room for ambiguity. A semiology of instructional arrows stands in for bombs or missiles: one arrow identifies the tank as belonging to the "Serbi," the other indicates it as the objective of the plane. The relationship between the two engines of destruction is as clear in its own way as that between the tank and the burning building. ■

LUFTË

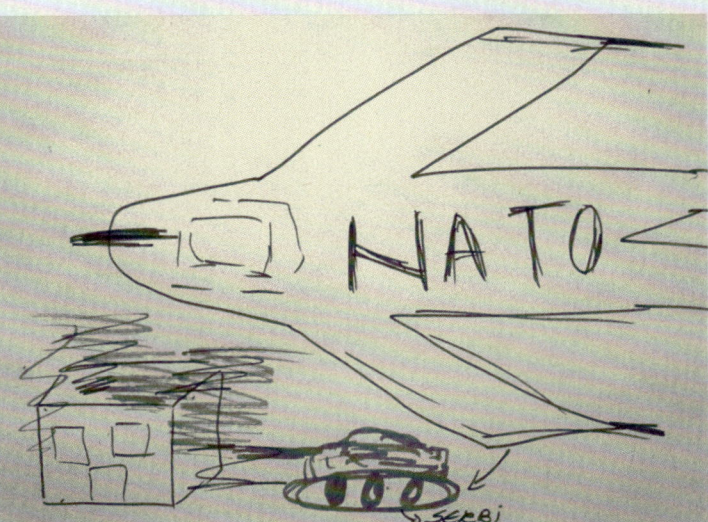

FIGURE 16
KOSOVAR GIRL (NAME WITHHELD)
AGE 16
DRAWN IN A REFUGEE CAMP
ALBANIA, 1999
DRAWING COURTESY OF KATHLEEN KING

36

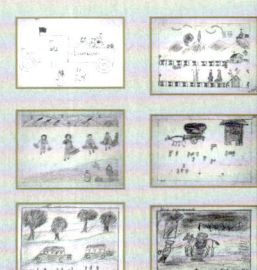
SEE COLOR PLATES PAGES 68–71

DISPLACEMENT
EVACUACIÓN **OPRÓŻNIENIE** EWAKUACJA

37

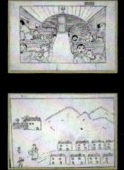

"I NOTICED THAT…MANY OF THE MOTHERS HAD TEARS IN THEIR EYES. HOW STRANGE, I THOUGHT, HOW STRANGE. OF COURSE, IT WASN'T LONG BEFORE I FOUND OUT WHY THEY WERE CRYING. THEY HAD PROPOSED TO ALL THE PARENTS THAT THOSE WHO WANTED COULD SEND THEIR CHILDREN OUT OF MADRID…."

FROM AN INTERVIEW WITH **ALFONSO ORTUÑO**
(COMPLETE INTERVIEW ON PAGE 76)

EVACUACIÓN

The Spanish Civil War displaced upwards of 200,000 children. In a number of drawings they depict scenes of their evacuation and flight.

Margarita García (age 10) drew this image of her evacuation (fig. 17 or plate 27). The truck, carefully drawn with a straight edge, holds five passengers and a minuscule driver, all sketched freehand. The central figure that immediately draws our eye is a weeping girl who we take to be Margarita, vastly larger than those who accompany her. Enormous tears roll down her face as she looks directly at us. Her sorrow dwarfs everything else. Two smaller figures, a mother and child, wave good-bye from the sidewalk, their backs to us. The woman next to them, face streaked with tears, one hand clasped to her mouth, faces us, a visual echo of the child in the truck. We can reasonably assume she is Margarita's mother. As in many children's drawings, here the exquisite detail of the large weeping face in contrast with the schematic rendering of the other figures (the driver is scarcely more than a stick figure) acquires great significance. Technical inexpertise and compositional errors carry meaning. There is no background, nothing to indicate location, whether city or country. There is only the sorrow of displacement. The lettering on the truck says it all: *"Evacuación."*

Other children depict their evacuation differently. If we cannot be sure exactly which of the figures represents the child artist in the preceding image, in this drawing Luisa Rodríguez, eleven years old, identifies herself, her mother, and her brother "as we were leaving for Santander. And the cannons shot shells that set Mt. Arraiz on fire," she wrote on the back of the picture (fig. 18 or plate 28). Five figures arrayed in a broad V walk toward the viewer. The children, eyes and mouths round with fear and wonder, carry their luggage. The mother's face is more serene or resigned, mouth and eyes elongated. In the background six schematically drawn houses, smoke rising from their chimneys, show us what they are leaving. Flames from the mountains on the back horizon show us why.

Teresa Vázquez (age 13), unlike the previous two child artists, shows no individuating features in her rendition of her evacuation (fig. 19 or plate 29). All the people, both those leaving and those bidding them farewell from the roadside, are tiny stick figures. The trees in the background loom over them. Hearselike vehicles transport the evacuees, whom we glimpse between the gathered curtains, as though clutched in the black teeth of a monster.

Yet another scene shows a family fleeing Irún into France (fig. 20 or plate 30). Fernando Olavera (age 13) has rendered the bridge, the border, and the refugee couple in great detail. The other elements—the border guards, other refugees, mountains and trees, the birds and sailboat—are sketched more schematically. The church or convent in the upper right-hand corner, though, received special attention. With the flattened perspective characteristic of children's art, and highlighted by its bright color, this building is nearly as large as the guard's shack in the foreground. The neatly lettered legend on the hill explains its significance: "San Marcial taken by the fascists," tracing a direct line of causality diagonally across the page. The refugees take flight because the fascists have occupied San Marcial. ■

CHILDREN OF THE SPANISH CIVIL WAR

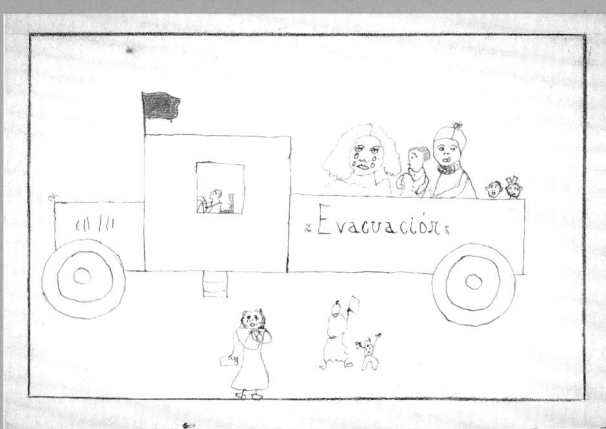

FIGURE 17
MARGARITA GARCÍA
AGE 10
SEE PLATE 27

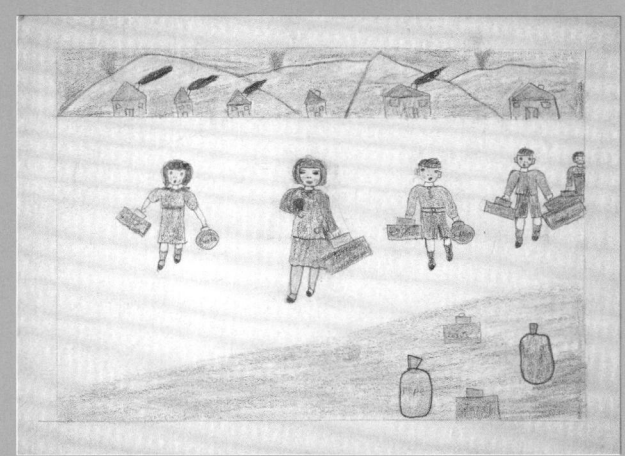

FIGURE 18
LUISA RODRÍGUEZ
AGE 11
SEE PLATE 28

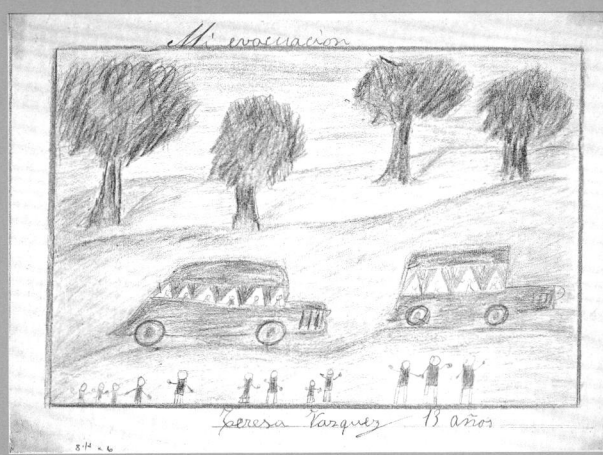

FIGURE 19
TERESA VÁZQUEZ
AGE 13
SEE PLATE 29

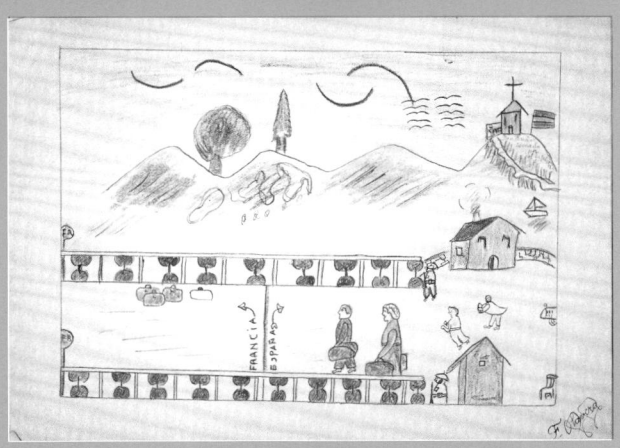

FIGURE 20
FERNANDO OLAVERA
AGE 13
SEE PLATE 30

40 — CHILDREN OF POLAND, 1939

OPRÓŻNIENIE

In the foreground (fig. 21) mounted soldiers—sabers drawn—chase and strike down unarmed civilians. A barbed wire fence, armed soldier blocking the only opening, separates this scene from the stationary train in the background. The boxcars, carefully outlined with a straight edge, stand in contrast with the hastily sketched soldiers who guard them.

Created by an anonymous young Polish deportee in 1939, after the partition of Poland by Nazi Germany and the Soviet Union, the drawing depicts Russian cavalry troops chasing civilians away from the train. In the caption that runs across the bottom of the picture, the child artist tells us, "We saw this sight from the train car!" The perspective is correct and realistic. The muted palette lends a somber, wintry feeling to the scene. Yet as we look more closely we realize that a curious shift in subject position has taken place. History has shown us, through countless documentary photos, films, and survivors' testimonies, that the civilians being deported to camps were *inside* the boxcars, behind those doors nailed shut with crossed timbers, in the background, confined by the barbed wire. But the child artist has positioned herself *outside* the scene, assuming the spectators' perspective and speaking collectively: "*We* saw this sight...."

How are we to understand this shift? Has she drawn herself into freedom? Has she moved next to us, the better for us to identify with her? Does she want to be closer to the scene of the beating of civilians, to bear witness? We shall never know, and we cannot ask her. What we do know is that she saw this through one of those tiny windows, high on the boxcar: "We saw this sight from the train car!" ■

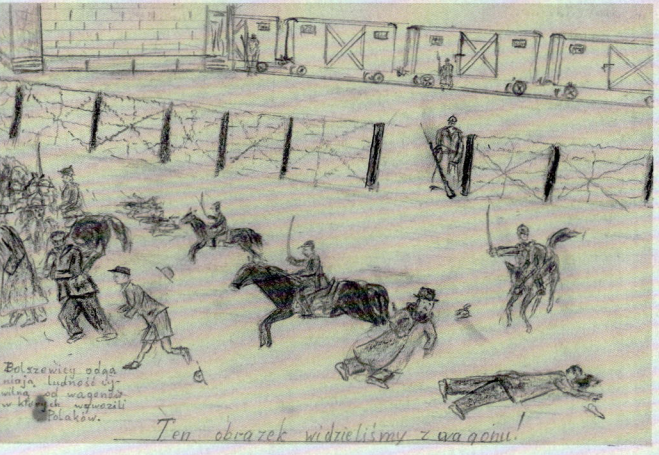

FIGURE 21
ANONYMOUS POLISH DEPORTEE
AGE UNKNOWN
1939
"BOLSHEVIKS CHASE CIVILIANS AWAY FROM THE TRAIN CARS IN WHICH THEY TOOK POLES AWAY."

DRAWING COURTESY OF THE HOOVER INSTITUTION FOR WAR, PEACE AND REVOLUTION

41

EWAKUACJA

CHILDREN OF SARAJEVO, 1992–1993

Rather than scenes of evacuation, these drawings, created by schoolchildren in Sarajevo in 1992, depict displacement. The savage interethnic warfare that wracked the former Yugoslavia less than a decade ago displaced thousands of civilians. Unlike the Spanish scenes of evacuation, which often depict the children's own experiences, these pictures feature adults: those intended to care for children are themselves represented as victims.

Saša, a sixth-grader, draws a group of adults, three women and two men, hiding in the forest (fig. 22). Child psychologists maintain that branches off the main trunk in children's artwork represent traumas experienced by the child. There is not a straight trunk in this picture. The refugees' torn and patched clothing not only tells of the hardship of life on the run but can be taken as a metaphor for their spiritual state. Their haunting expressions are rendered identically: foreheads and cheeks deeply lined, eyes and brows cast at the same angle, mouths set in sorrow. The exquisitely realistic detail of the stubble on the men's cheeks captures their fragility and desolation. At the same time, each face is individual, suggesting that the collective tragedy is also always experienced personally.

Vanja, also a sixth-grader, draws naked, skeletal figures in an irregularly shaped barbed wire enclosure, which is brightly illuminated, as though under a spotlight (fig. 23). All seven cast a shadow. It is a statement without context; we do not know who the prisoners are or why they are confined. The cartoon-like figures have an enormous expressive power, reduced as they are to their essential humanity: eyes round in fear, mouths open, ribs protruding, flesh exposed. The young artist has captured a poignant detail: the glasses worn by the figure on the far left suggest greater vulnerability. They both shield his eyes and allow him to see. They are all he has left of civilized life outside the enclosure. ■

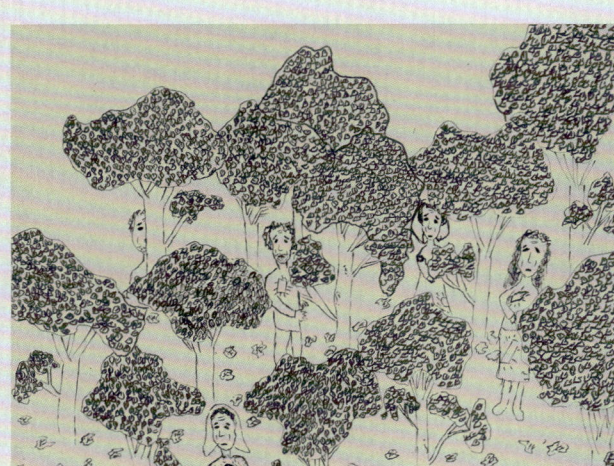

FIGURE 22
SAŠA
AGE UNKNOWN, SIXTH GRADE
SARAJEVO, 1992

COURTESY OF THE SAN FRANCISCO INTERNATIONAL
CHILDREN'S ART MUSEUM

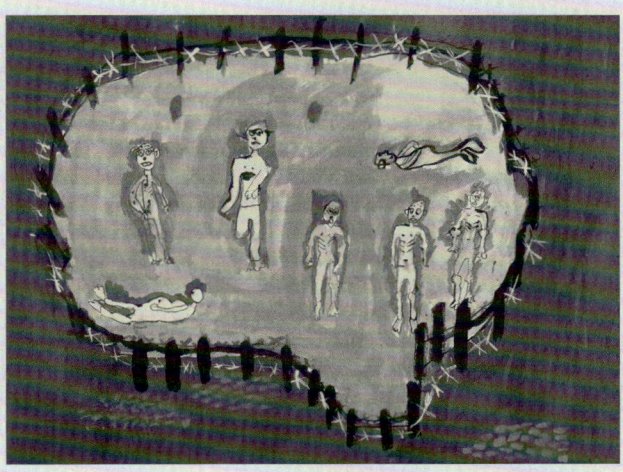

FIGURE 23
VANJA
AGE UNKNOWN, SIXTH GRADE
SARAJEVO, 1992

COURTESY OF THE SAN FRANCISCO INTERNATIONAL
CHILDREN'S ART MUSEUM

42

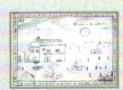 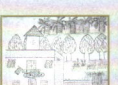 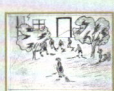 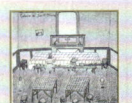

SEE COLOR PLATES PAGES 72–73

CAMPS
COLONIAS **LOGOR** LAGER

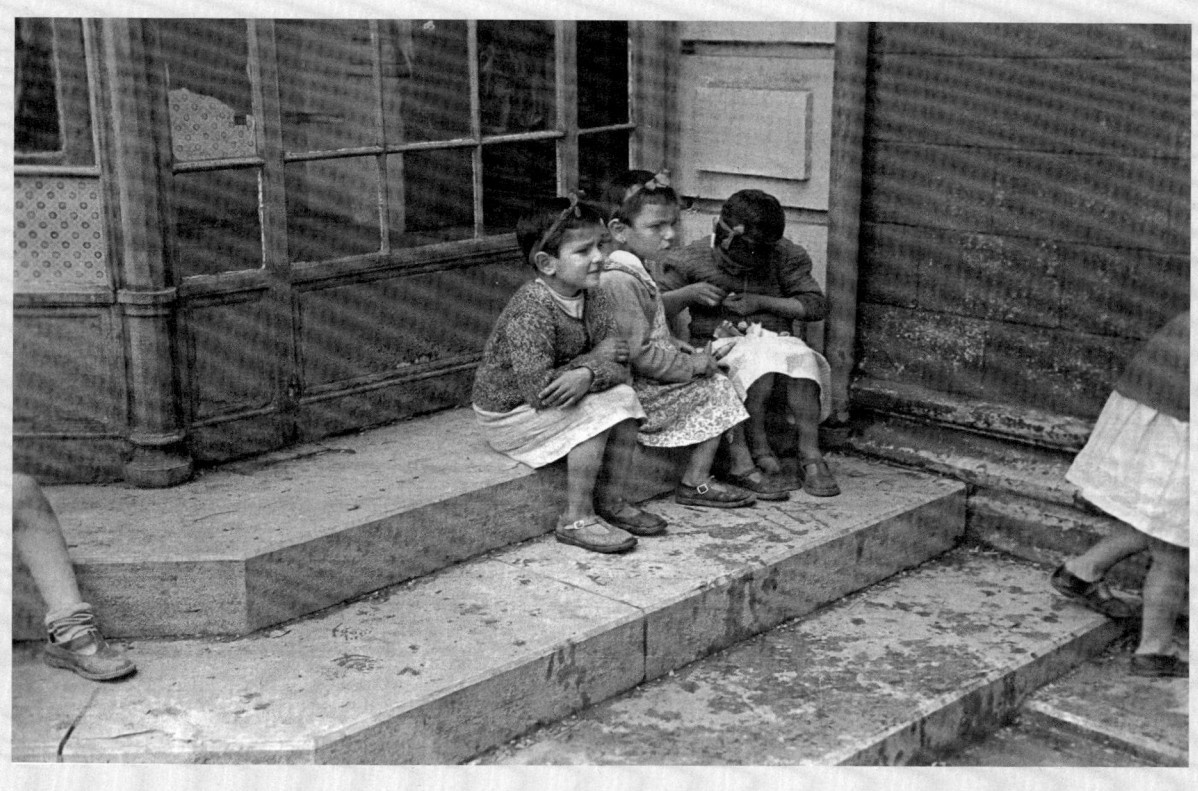
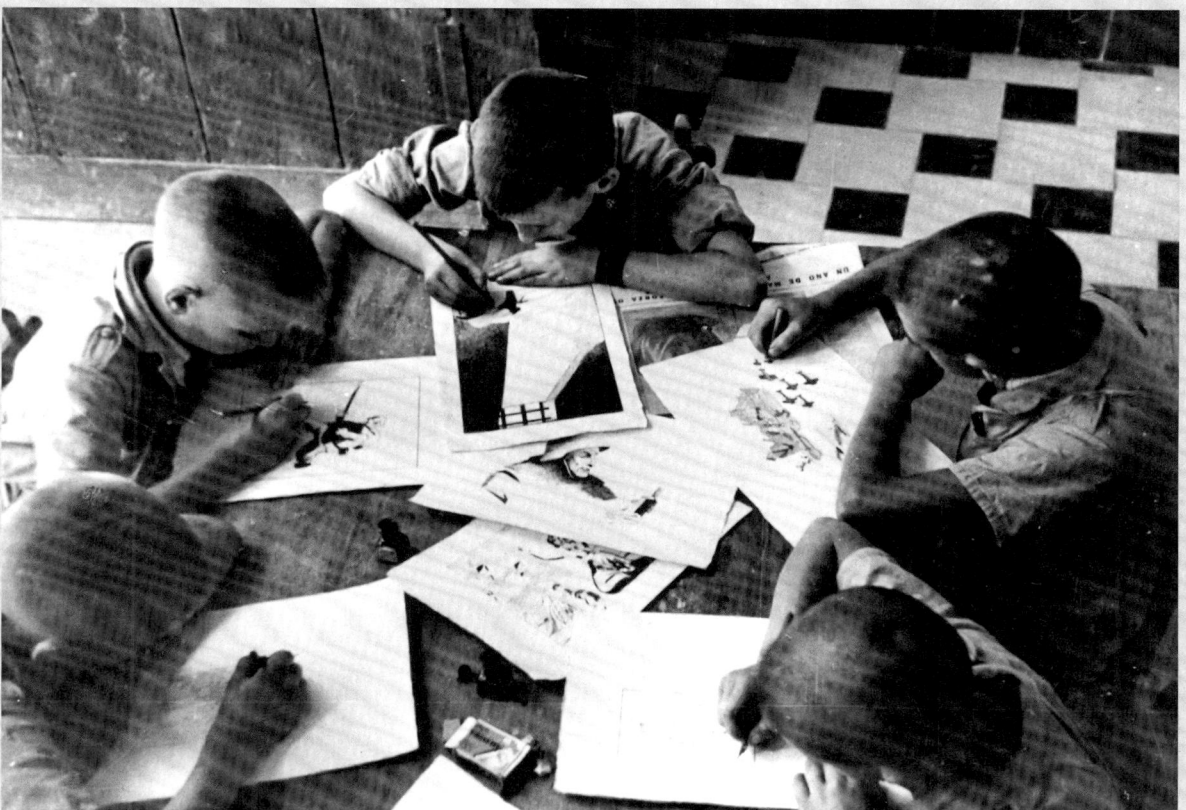

44

COLONIAS

"THE CHILDREN LIVE HERE WITH TEACHERS, COOKS, NURSES, IN THE PROPORTION OF ONE ADULT TO FIVE CHILDREN AND USUALLY TEN TO FIFTY CHILDREN IN ONE HOUSE. [...] GREAT INDIVIDUALITY MARKS THE LIFE IN THESE COLONIES WHICH FOLLOW THE EDUCATIONAL IDEALS OF THE TEACHER IN CHARGE. [...] MOST OF ALL, I WAS STRUCK BY THE QUALITY OF THE CHILDREN [...]"

PREVIOUS PAGE

FIGURE 24
PHOTOGRAPH BY ROBERT CAPA
NEAR BIARRITZ, FRANCE
MAY 1939
COURTESY OF CORNELL CAPA

FIGURE 25
CHILDREN DRAWING IN A COLONY
PHOTOGRAPH COURTESY OF THE BUTLER LIBRARY
(COLUMBIA UNIVERSITY)

GEIST

After the grim realities of war depicted in these drawings it comes as a relief to know that the children who had witnessed such horrors could also produce visions of joy. One of the topics that their teachers frequently assigned was scenes of life in the colonies. Far from the front, the government-sponsored group homes offered comfort and security after the trauma of bombardment, death, and displacement. In 1937 the American journalist Anna Louise Strong described the colonies:

(Strong, in Collins 10).

Capa, too, was struck by the almost utopian nature of the colonies, as we see in the photographs he took in a home for Republican orphans near Biarritz in 1939. Unlike the isolation of the children whom he photographed on the move a few months earlier and not far from these scenes, here we see the children in groups. In one, three girls sit close together, in the protection of domestic walls and windows (fig. 24). Their expressions and body language suggest security and comfort rather than solitude. In another, reminiscent of some of Matisse's late cutouts and collages, Capa captures the grace and beauty of girls dancing (fig. 31).

Jesús Ezquerro Ruiz's drawing of children in the colony contains virtually all the elements of a happy child's representation of his world: mountains, trees, a house, smoke billowing from the chimney, children at play, and a humanized sun watching benevolently over it (fig. 26 or plate 35). Turtles paddle in the fountain. Tiny figures jump rope, work in the garden, play soccer. The ten-year-old artist represents life in the colony as collective. The children have no individuating features but live and work in harmony, their identity collective. An ornate border bounds the picture, as though setting it off from the world outside the colony.

In Natalio Gómez Martín's depiction of life in the colony, he pays much greater attention to the detail of the building and grounds than to the colony's inhabitants (fig. 27 or plate 36). Note the carefully traced roof tiles, the clock that marks half past two, the wrought iron grillwork of the windows and fence in the foreground. In the background a line of meticulously drawn palm trees indicates the horizon. Somewhat closer another row of trees—poplars perhaps—neatly arranged and nearly identical, parallels the palms. Everything suggests order, solidity, stability. These are the boundaries of the colony. At their center, held in their embrace, tiny stick figures swim in a pool. Their diminutive size does not suggest vulnerability, as in a number of other drawings we have seen, where the sheer power of destruction dwarfs any human scale. Rather, here it is the structures of their protection that are unnaturally large.

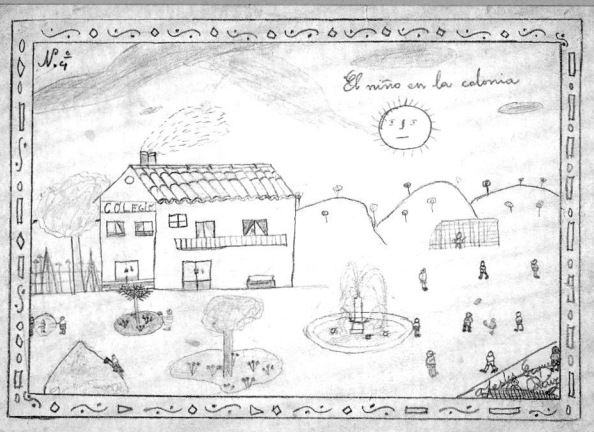

FIGURE 26
JESÚS EZQUERRO RUIZ,
AGE 10
SEE PLATE 35

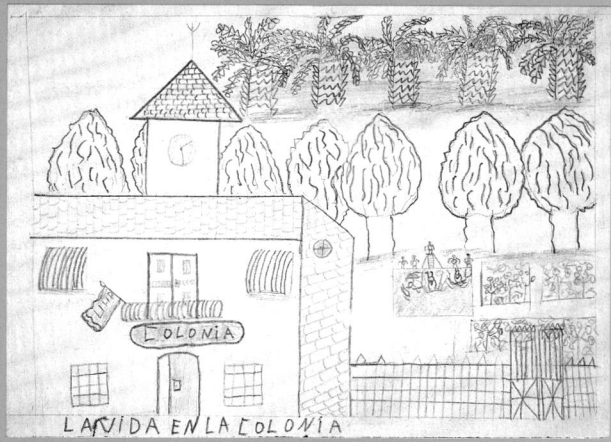

FIGURE 27
NATALIO GÓMEZ MARTÍN
AGE 14
SEE PLATE 36

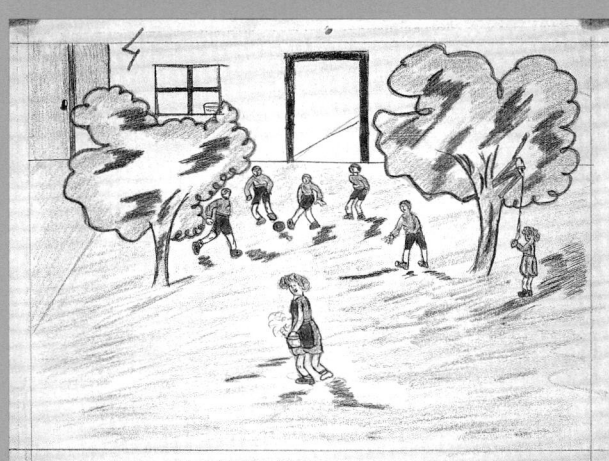

FIGURE 28
ÁNGELES ARNÁIZ
AGE 14
SEE PLATE 37

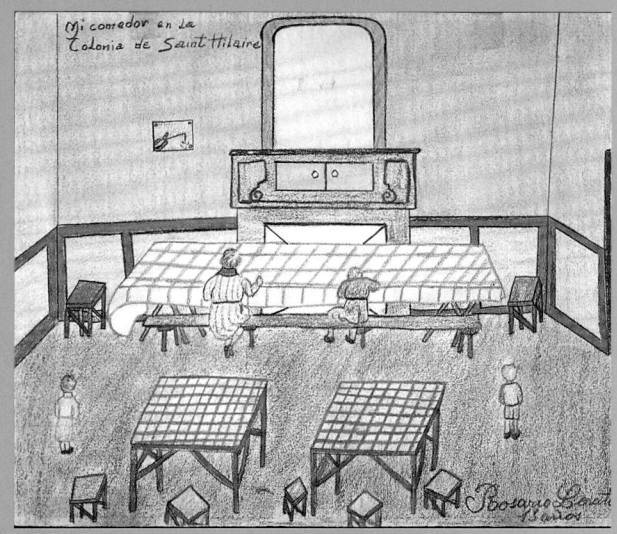

FIGURE 29
ROSARIO LORATE
AGE 13
SEE PLATE 38

Ángeles Arnáiz (age 14) shows a detail of life in the Colonia Infantil de Bayona (France) (fig. 28 or plate 37). She explains on the back of the picture that she has drawn herself ringing the lunch bell as the cook carries a pot of stew across the courtyard. Five boys are playing soccer. Note the symmetry of the drawing, the open door to the colony squarely centered in the back, two large trees holding the ballplayers in a protective embrace. The composition suggests order, play, nourishment, and security.

Finally, the exact symmetry with which Rosario Lorate represents the dining room at her colony speaks to us of order, stability, harmony (fig. 29 or plate 38). Notice that at the age of thirteen she has mastered perspective. ■

THE FOLLOWING EXTRACT APPEARED AS AN ARTICLE: DOROTHY PARKER, "NO AXE TO GRIND," VOLUNTEER FOR LIBERTY, VOL. I, NO. 23, MADRID, NOVEMBER 15, 1937.

The Government takes care, too, of the unfortunate of the war. There are a million refugee children in Spain. A million is an easy number to say. But how can you grasp what it means? Three hundred thousand of them are in the homes of families and seven hundred thousand are in children's colonies. When it can, the Government wants to have all in colonies. I hope that will happen, because I have seen some of the colonies. There is no dreadful orphan asylum quality about them. I never saw finer children—free and growing and happy. One colony was in a sea-side resort, near Valencia. There were sixty children, from four to fourteen, who had been going to a school in Madrid.
And the Fascist planes bombed the school….

It was amazing to see how many of these children could draw and draw well—and it was heartening to see how their talent was encouraged by the teachers. When they first came to the colony, the children drew the things that were nearest and deepest to them—they drew planes and bursting bombs and houses in flames. You could see by the dreadful perfection of detail, how well they knew their subjects. Now they are drawing flowers and apples and sail boats and little houses with smoke coming out of the chimneys. They are well children now.

And in Valencia, a few miles away, the Fascist planes come over and the bombs drop, and so there will be more children who will draw planes and flames and fragments of bodies blown into the air. That is if there are any children left….

47

CAMPS

CHILDREN OF THE JAPANESE AMERICAN INTERNMENT CAMP, TANFORAN, CALIFORNIA, 1942

As Americans we tend to think of the trauma of war as a sorrow visited upon children of other lands, overseas, distant from us. Yet in 1942 and 1943 thousands of American citizens and legal residents of Japanese ancestry, mostly on the West Coast, were rounded up and sent to internment camps for the duration of the war. Many lost their property, jobs, businesses, homes. Some young men were released into military service in the European theater.

Among those interned were numerous children. Contemporary accounts inform us that in the camps—usually located in inhospitable arid regions far from the coast—the children went to school, formed baseball teams, followed teenage fashion as best they could, and, at least in some camps, drew pictures as well.

Before the war, Chiura Obata was a popular professor of art at the University of California at Berkeley, a position to which he returned after his release. He was first interned at Tanforan, just over the hills south of San Francisco. Tanforan—then a horseracing track, today a suburban shopping center—was a staging area from which Japanese American detainees were relocated to internment camps farther inland, in California, Nevada, Idaho, Utah, and Montana. Obata was transferred from Tanforan to Topaz, Utah, where he was confined with his family and over 8,000 other Japanese Americans. There he founded the Topaz Art School and organized sixteen other artist instructors to give art classes to over 600 children.

This watercolor, unsigned, was painted by one of those children. The wash technique is sophisticated, the perspective accurate. A high barbed wire fence separates the foreground from the grain warehouse and numbered barracks in the background. Barren hills appear between the buildings. It is difficult to ascertain how much the somber mood of the painting owes to traditional Japanese sumi-e ink technique, but the absolute absence of any sign of human life gives it an air of desolation. There is not even any smoke in the chimney. The telephone wires, promising communication with the outside world, pass over the camp. The difference from Spanish children's depiction of life in the *colonias* could not be greater. ∎

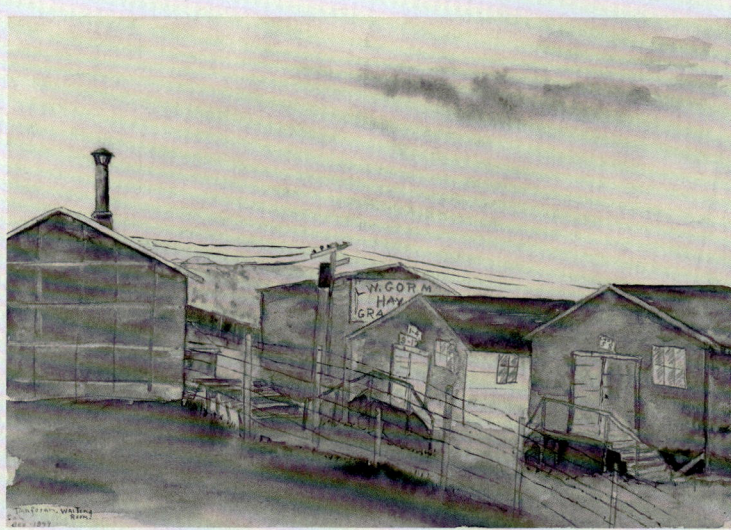

FIGURE 30
ARTIST UNKNOWN
TANFORAN, CALIF., C. 1942

DRAWING COURTESY OF THE NATIONAL
JAPANESE AMERICAN HISTORICAL SOCIETY

48

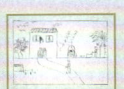 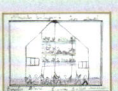 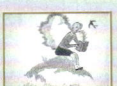 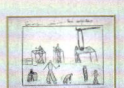

SEE COLOR PLATES PAGES 74–75

PEACE
PAZ FRIEDEN **PAIX** SHALOM **SALAAM**

49

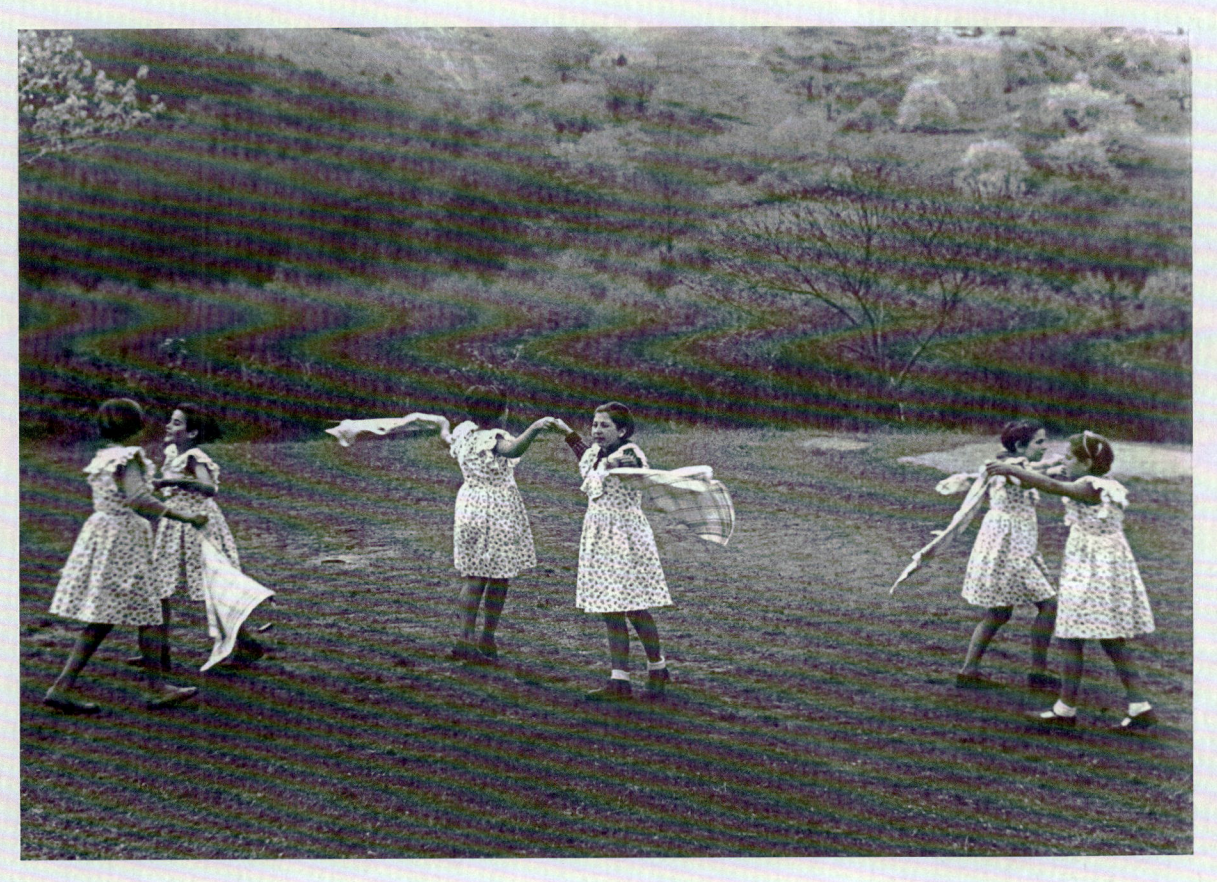

PAZ

GEIST

Finally, I would like to conclude with three visions of the future. Carmen Sierra (age 12) draws an idyllic country scene (fig. 32 or plate 39). Smoke flows reassuringly from the chimney of a house. Over the door the name PEPA identifies it or its occupant. Birds, not bombers, fill the sky as trees recede in orderly rows behind the house and well. To the left a tree stands laden with fruit. To the right, a woman (Pepa?) washes clothes under a palm tree. Whimsically, a dog quacks ("*Cuá*") at the mailman approaching with a letter in his hand. Everything is in its place.

Nine-year-old Emilio Díaz Luna depicts masons at work (fig. 33 or plate 40). "I will be a mason," he affirms in strong lettering. A large crew of workmen erect a house, working in concert. After so many buildings in flames or rubble, he will build or rebuild, constructing the future.

Ten-year-old Felisa Blanco's subject sits on a grassy knoll, book open in her hands (fig. 34 or plate 41). Light bursts through the clouds that form a nimbus around her as the dove of peace flies past. The child reader is well clothed and serene, in a future that brings peace, culture, and the well-being of children together in a vision of harmony. Yet we have no way of knowing if Felisa ever saw this dream realized.

What gives these pictures a special poignancy that transcends our own children's artistic efforts, fixed with magnets on refrigerator doors, is our knowledge of the special circumstances in which they were drawn. Born of the trauma of exile and separation, the drawings are invaluable historical documents, picturing for us the effects of the Spanish Civil War on its youngest victims. At the same time, they stand as testimony to the human spirit in the face of adversity. The meanings we derive from the variety of styles, skills, and subjects in the drawings from the Republican *colonias infantiles* spring from what Cary Nelson calls the "complex negotiations between experience and multiple forms of representation" (1996, 24).

Adult representations of children are commonplace, from the iconography of the Spanish Civil War to today's debates over abortion issues and welfare reform. Those images are often effective political tools. Yet the drawings from the colonies open a window onto children's subjectivity in ways that other artistic expressions cannot. Federico García Lorca, himself the victim of a Falangist firing squad in 1936, wrote a few years before the war that the child "understands better than we the ineffable key to poetic substance" (in Stainton 198). That poetry lives on, despite overwhelming odds, in the children's ability to still draw pictures. ■

PREVIOUS PAGE

FIGURE 24
PHOTOGRAPH BY ROBERT CAPA
NEAR BIARRITZ, FRANCE
MAY 1939
COURTESY OF CORNELL CAPA

51

CHILDREN OF THE SPANISH CIVIL WAR

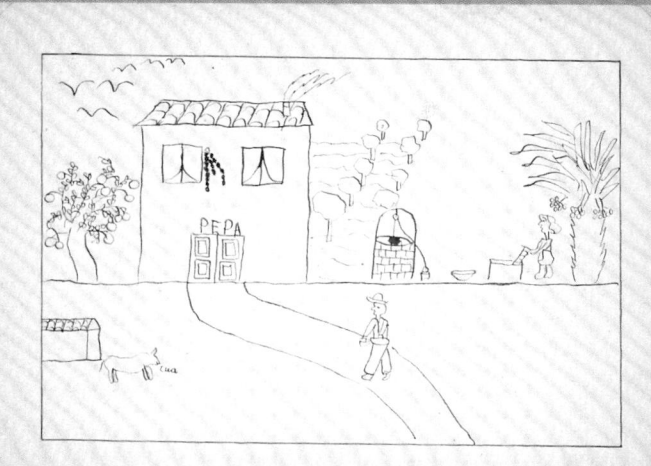

FIGURE 32
CARMEN SIERRA
AGE 12
SEE PLATE 39

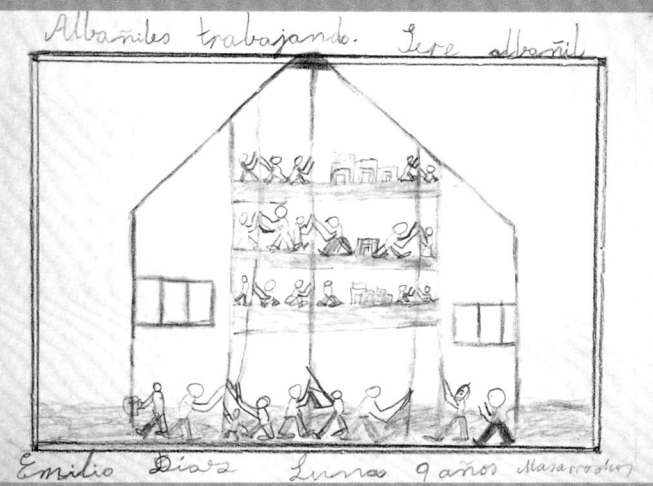

FIGURE 33
EMILIO DÍAZ LUNA
AGE 9
SEE PLATE 40

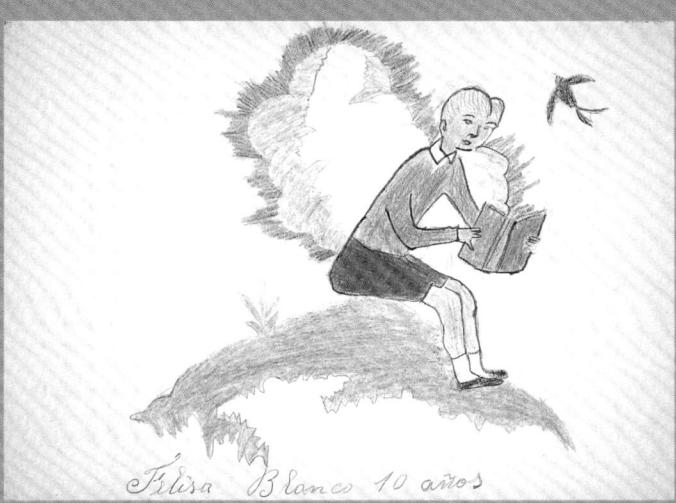

FIGURE 34
FELISA BLANCO
AGE 10
SEE PLATE 41

BIBLIOGRAPHY

Robert Capa, *Heart of Spain: Robert Capa's Photographs of the Spanish Civil War*. New York: Aperture / Madrid: Museo Nacional Centro de Arte Reina Sofía, 1999.

George R. and Christiane Crasemann Collins, "Children's Drawings of the Spanish Civil War," in *Children's Drawings of the Spanish Civil War*. New York: The Spanish Institute, 1986. 8–26.

Ernest Hemingway, *For Whom the Bell Tolls*. New York: Charles Scribner, 1996.

Aldous Huxley, *They Still Draw Pictures*. New York: Spanish Child Welfare Association of America for the American Friends Service Committee, 1938.

Virginia Malbin, "Case Record of New Spain," *Social Work Today* (November–December 1937), 9–11.

Cary Nelson, "Nightmares of Dead Children, Dreams of Utopia: Posters of the 1936–1939 Spanish Civil War," in Susan Martin and Pilar Pérez, eds., *Blood Sweat and Tears*. Los Angeles: Smart Art Press, 1997. 4–8.

Cary Nelson, *Shouts from the Wall: Posters and Photographs Brought Home from the Spanish Civil War by American Volunteers*. Waltham, Mass.: Abraham Lincoln Brigade Archives, 1996.

Leslie Stainton, *Lorca: A Dream of Life*. New York: Farrar, Straus & Giroux, 1999.

Nicholas Stargardt, "Children's Art of the Holocaust," *Past and Present* (November 1998).

Hugh Thomas, *The Spanish Civil War*. New York, Evanston, and London: Harper Colophon Books, 1963.

53

COLOR PLATES

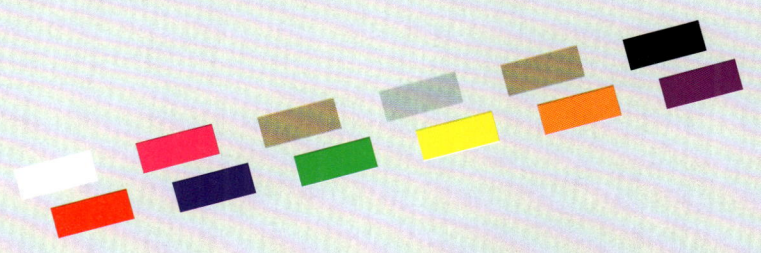

BEFORE: MEMORIES OF LOSS

PLATE 1
CARMEN SIERRA
AGE 12
MINISTERIO DE
INSTRUCCIÓN PÚBLICA,
RESIDENCIA INFANTIL Nº 20
TANGEL (ALICANTE)

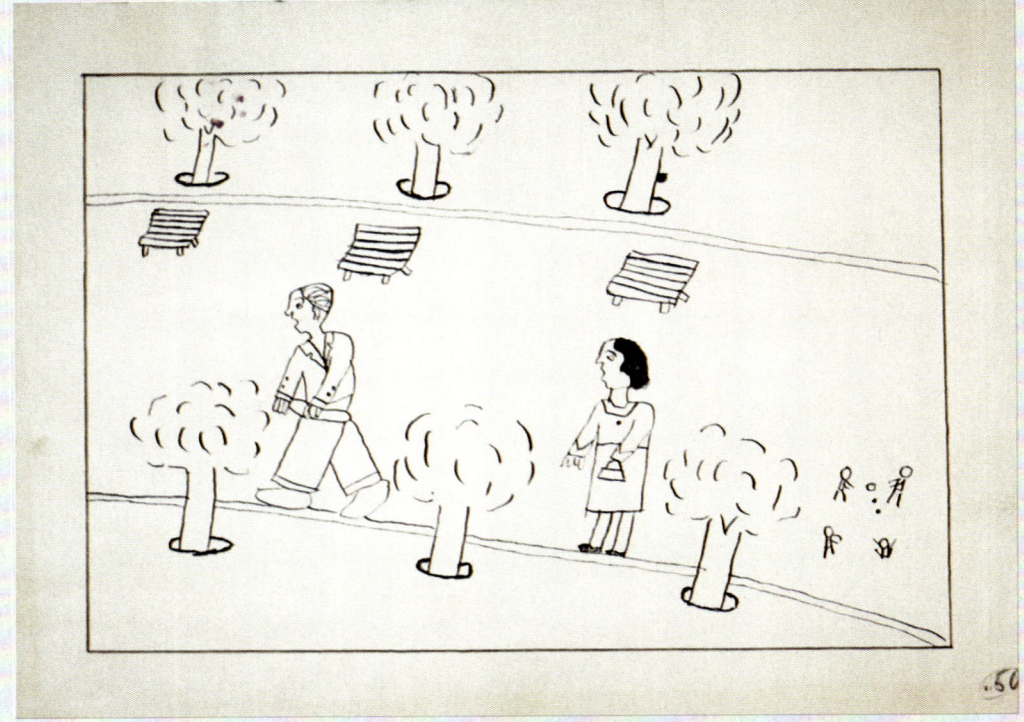

PLATE 2
LUIS VERGARA
AGE 11
MINISTERIO DE
INSTRUCCIÓN PÚBLICA,
COLONIA ESCOLAR Nº 1
TORRENTE (VALENCIA)

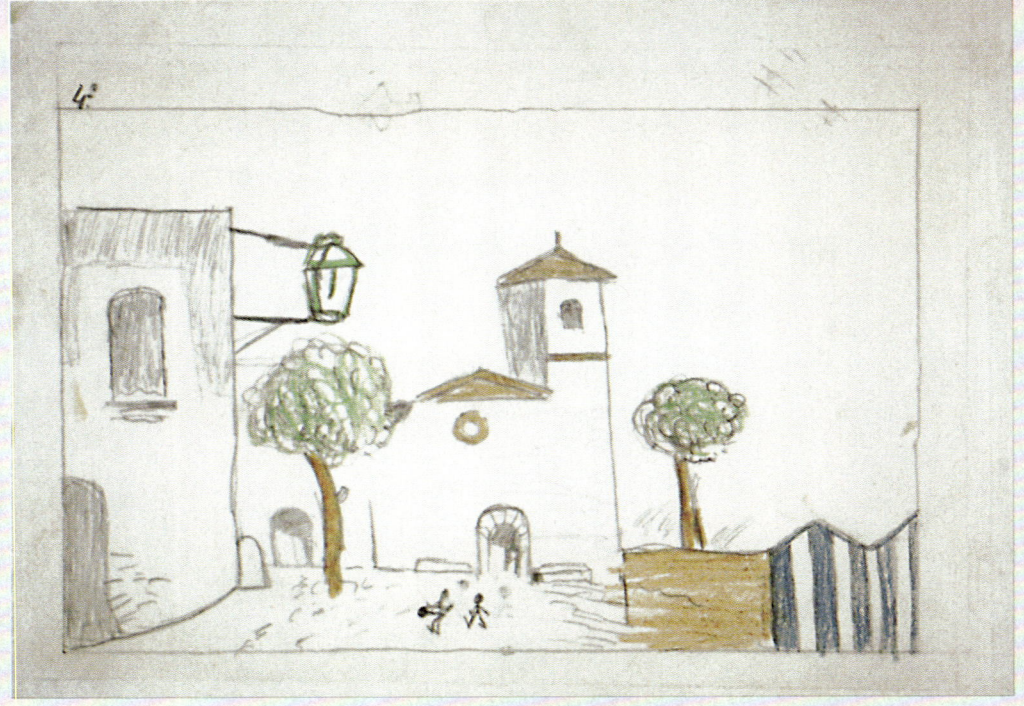

BEFORE: MEMORIES OF LOSS

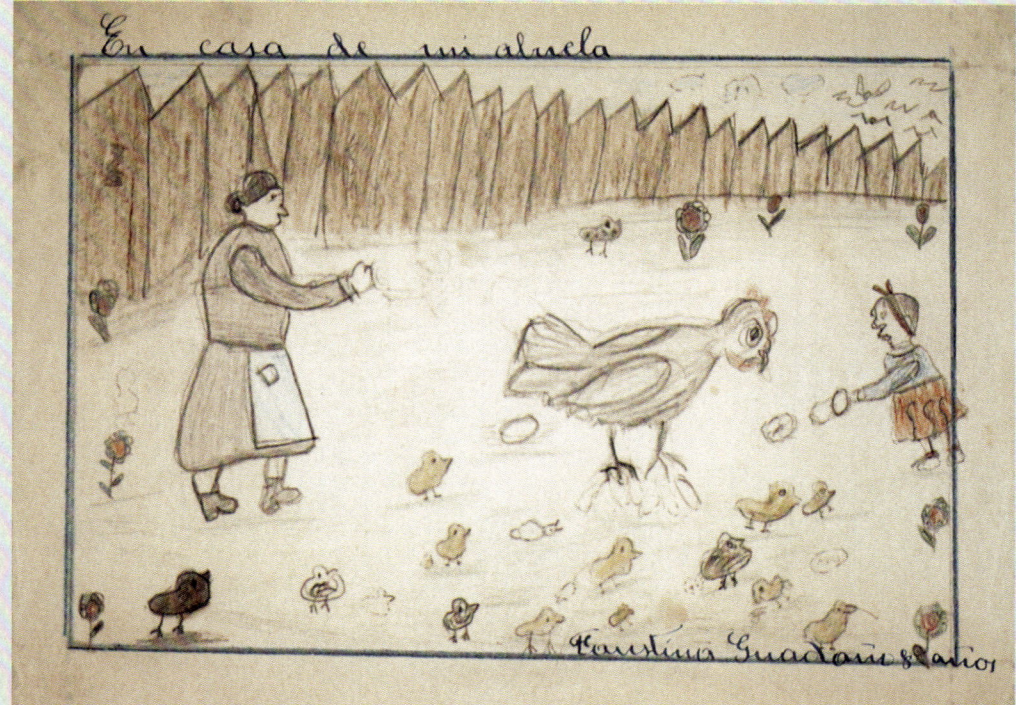

PLATE 3
FAUSTINA GUADAÑO
AGE 8
MASARROCHOS (VALENCIA)
"AT MY GRANDMOTHER'S HOUSE"
VERSO: "BEFORE THE WAR"

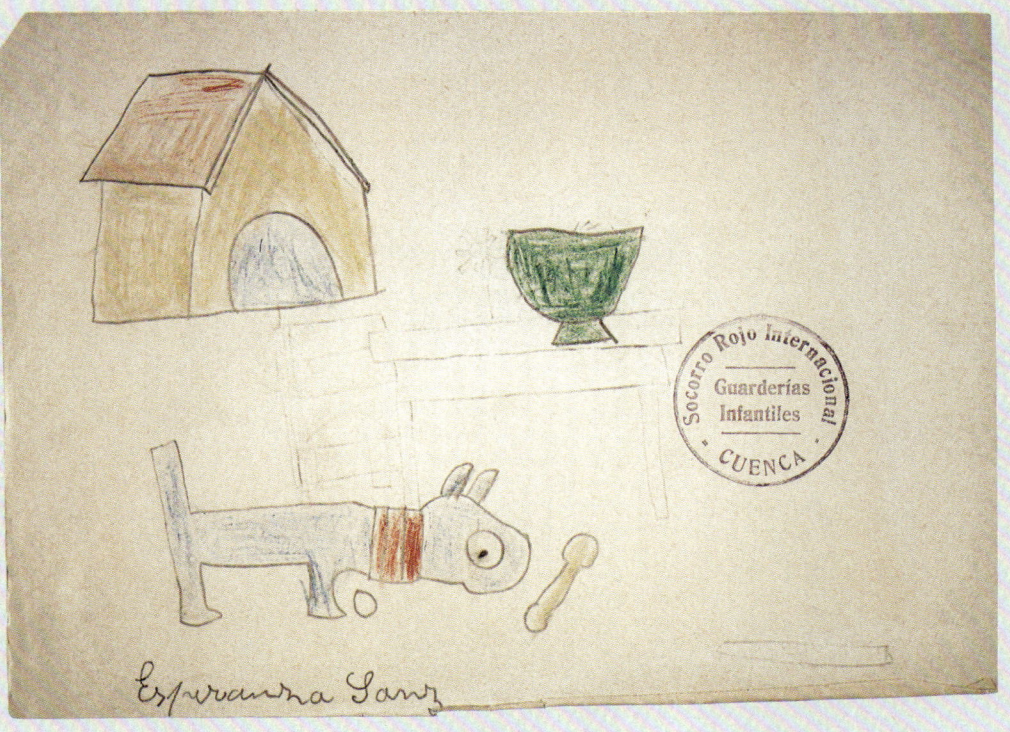

PLATE 4
ESPERANZA SANZ
AGE UNKNOWN
SOCORRO ROJO INTERNACIONAL, GUARDERÍAS INFANTILES (CUENCA)

BEFORE: MEMORIES OF LOSS

PLATE 5
ALEJANDRO CHILIÁN
AGE 11
INSTITUTO-ESCUELA DE 2º ENSEÑANZA,
VALENCIA
"PEACETIME"

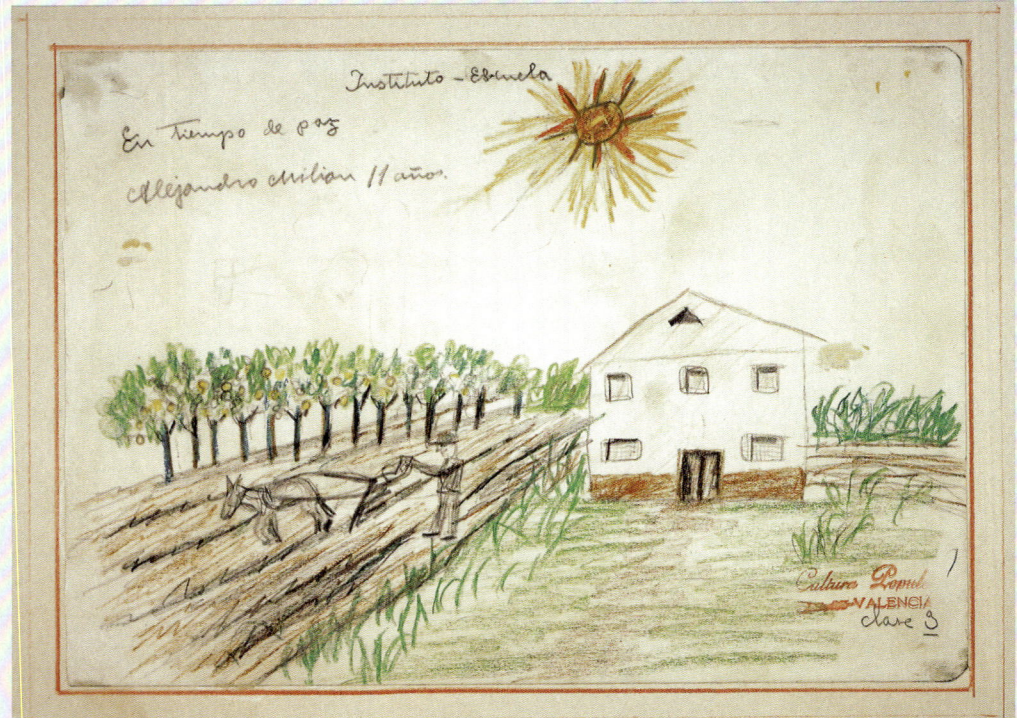

PLATE 6
PILAR GUMIEL MIGUEL
AGE 13
RESIDENCIA INFANTIL Nº 3
VILLAJOYOSA (ALICANTE)
"GOING OUT FISHING"

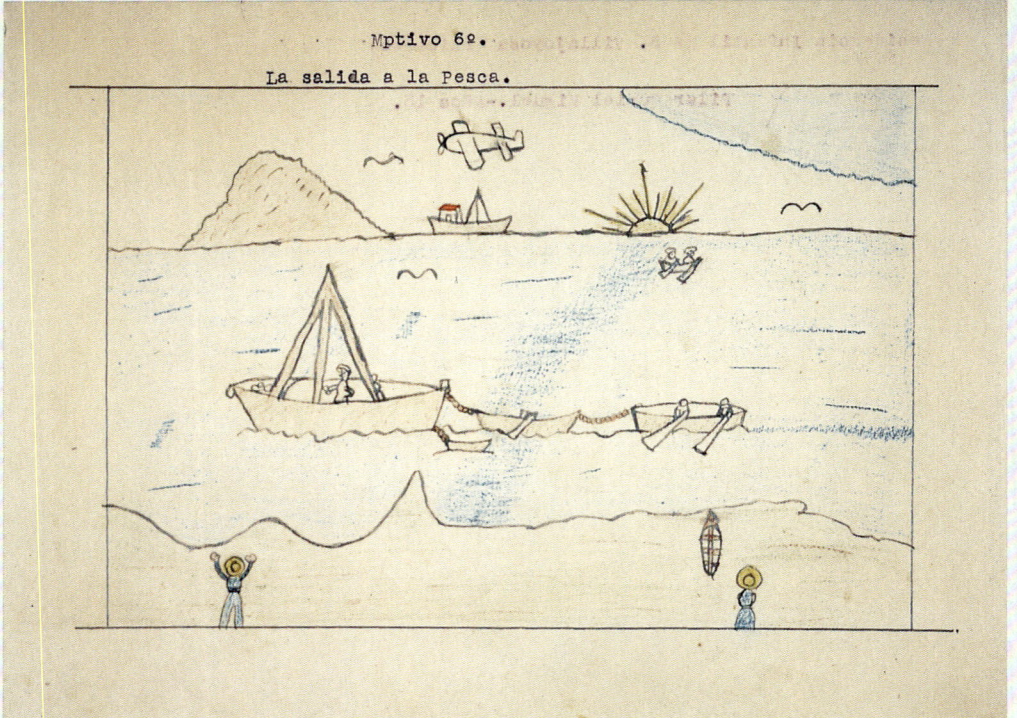

BEFORE: MEMORIES OF LOSS

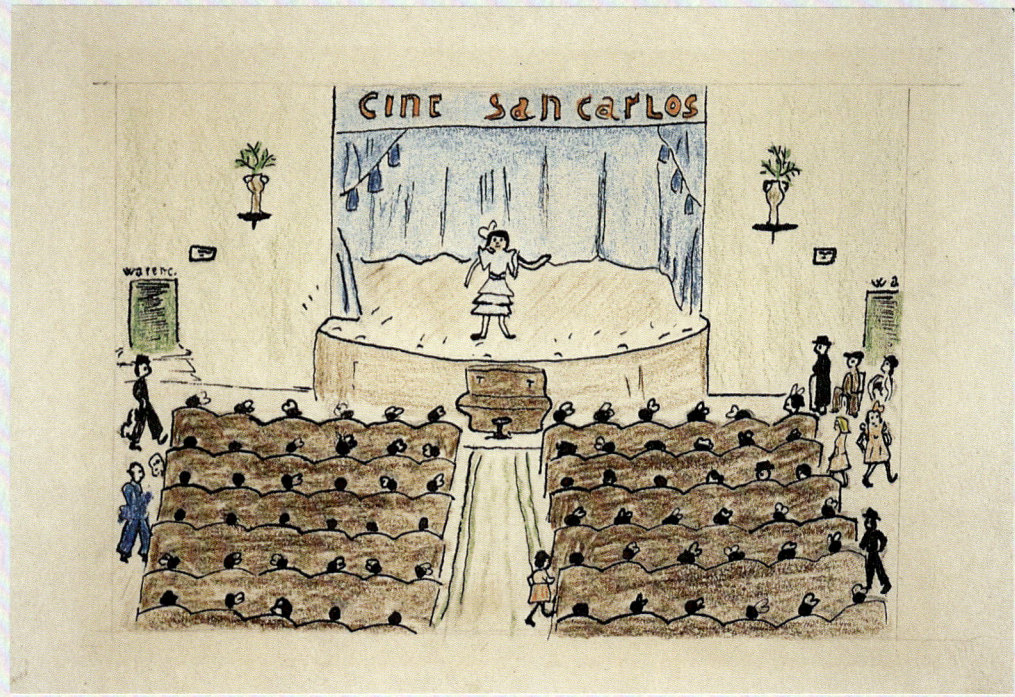

PLATE 7
ARTIST UNKNOWN
AGE UNKNOWN
COLONIA ESCOLAR BELLÚS (VALENCIA)
"SAN CARLOS THEATER"

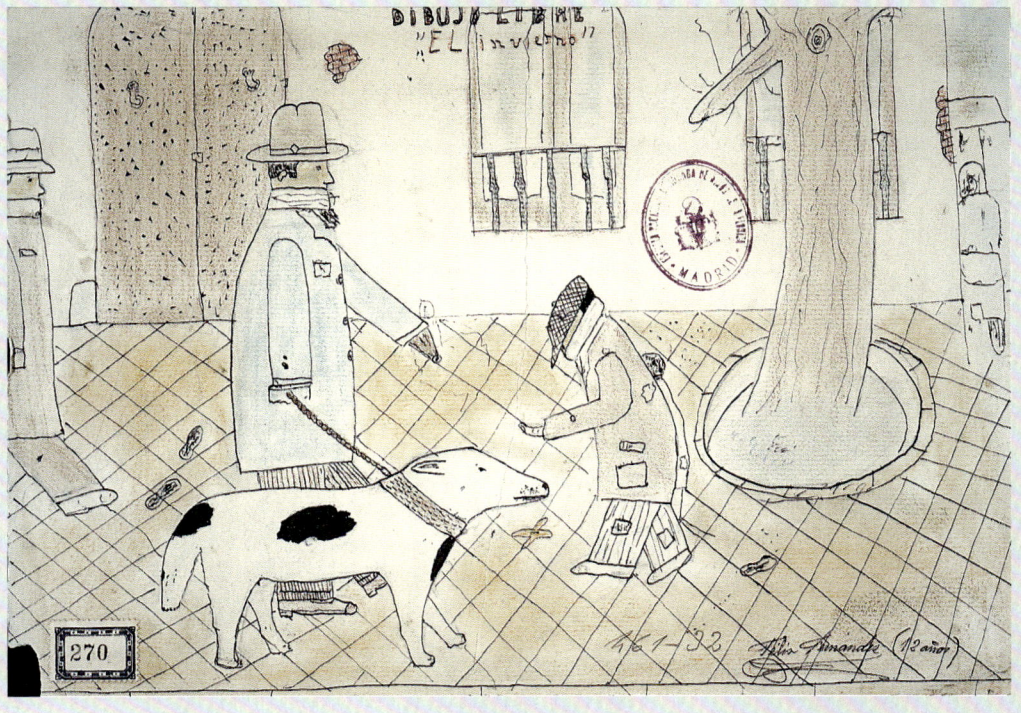

PLATE 8
FÉLIX FERNÁNDEZ
AGE 12
ESCUELA NACIONAL GRADUADA DE NIÑOS DE LA FLORIDA, MADRID
"WINTER"

58 WAR

PLATE 9
RAFAEL BARBER
AGE 10
COLONIA ESCOLAR
COLECTIVA
BURRIANA (CASTELLÓN)

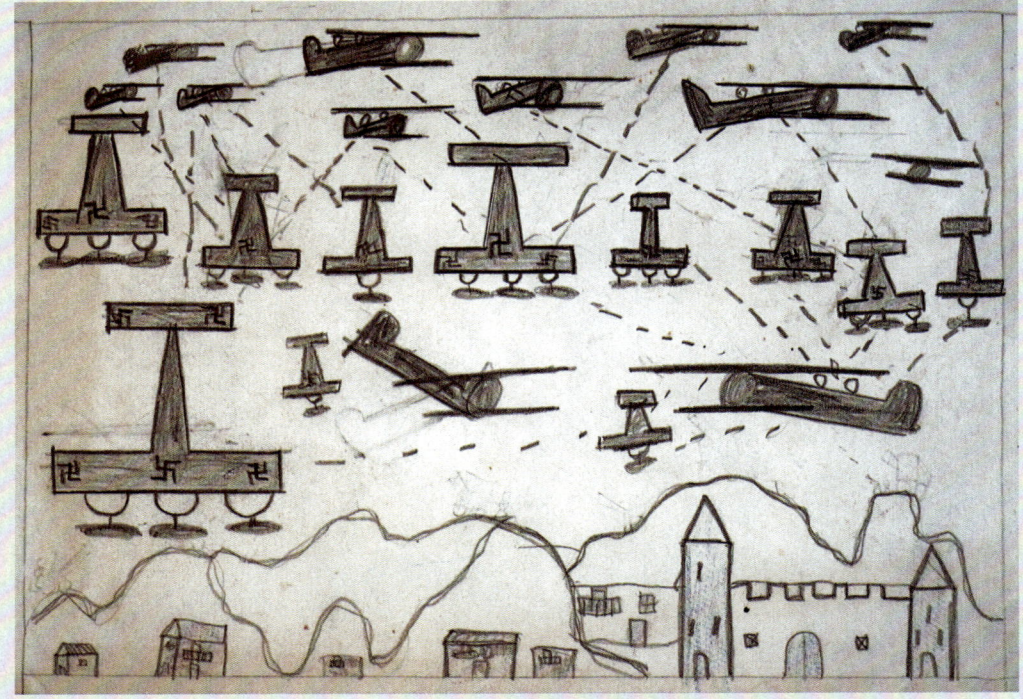

PLATE 10
MIGUEL ERCAÑO GARCÍA
AGE 12
UNIDENTIFIED LOCALE

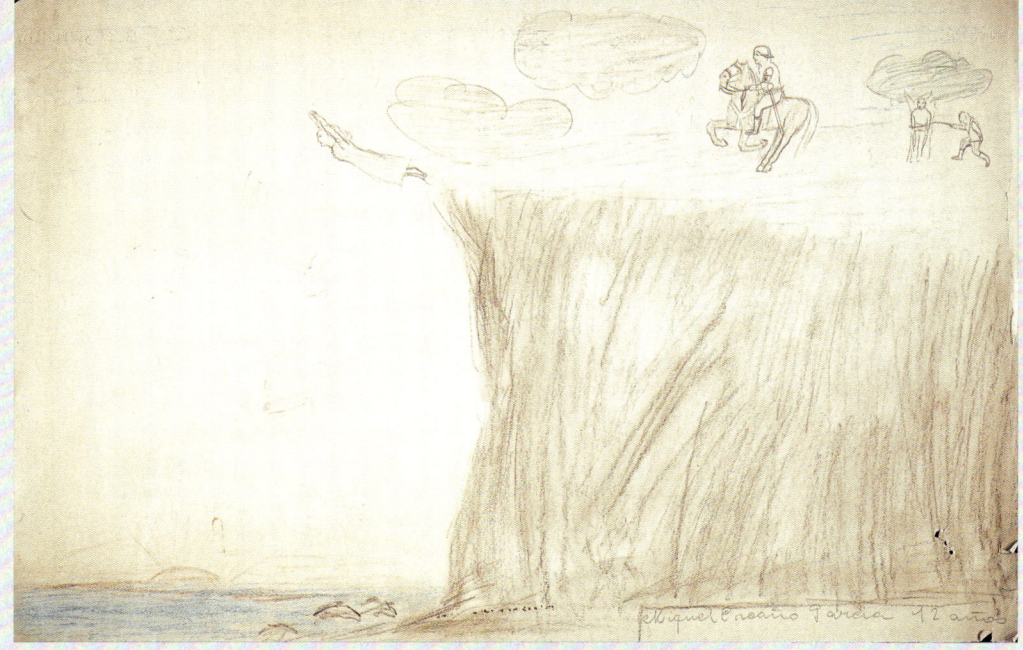

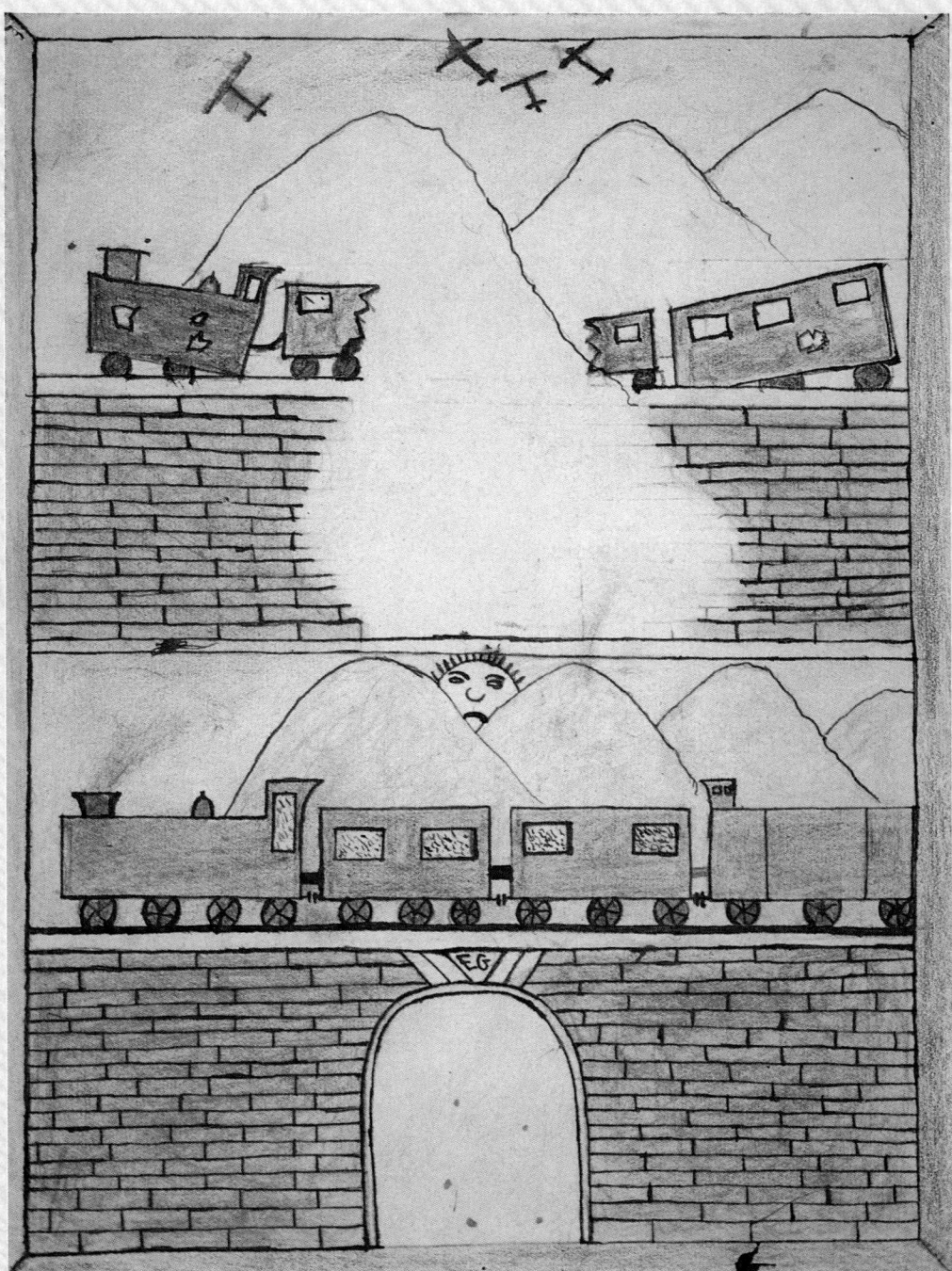

PLATE 11
E.G.
AGE UNKNOWN
RESIDENCIAS INFANTILES,
COLONIA DE EL ALBA
ONTENIENTE (VALENCIA)

PLATE 12
MARGARITA ARNAO CRESPO
AGE 12
COLONIA ESCOLAR
COLECTIVA LA TORRE
BENEJAMA (ALICANTE)

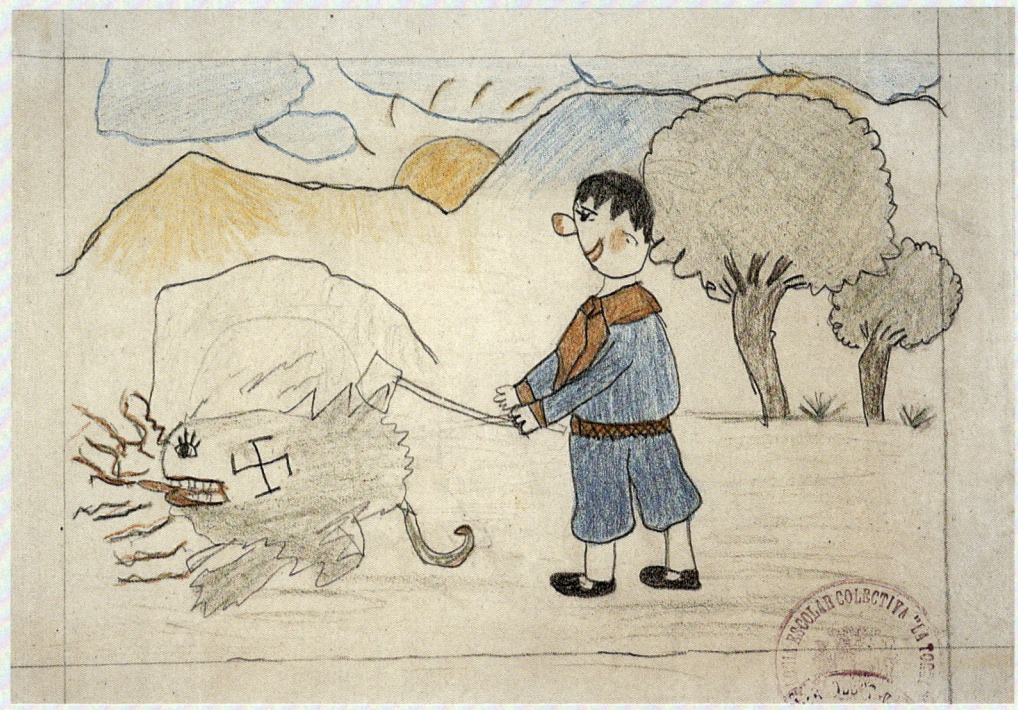

PLATE 13
VICENTE TEROL ROMEROS
AGE 14
VALENCIA, JANUARY 22, 1938
"SINKING OF THE 'SPAIN'"

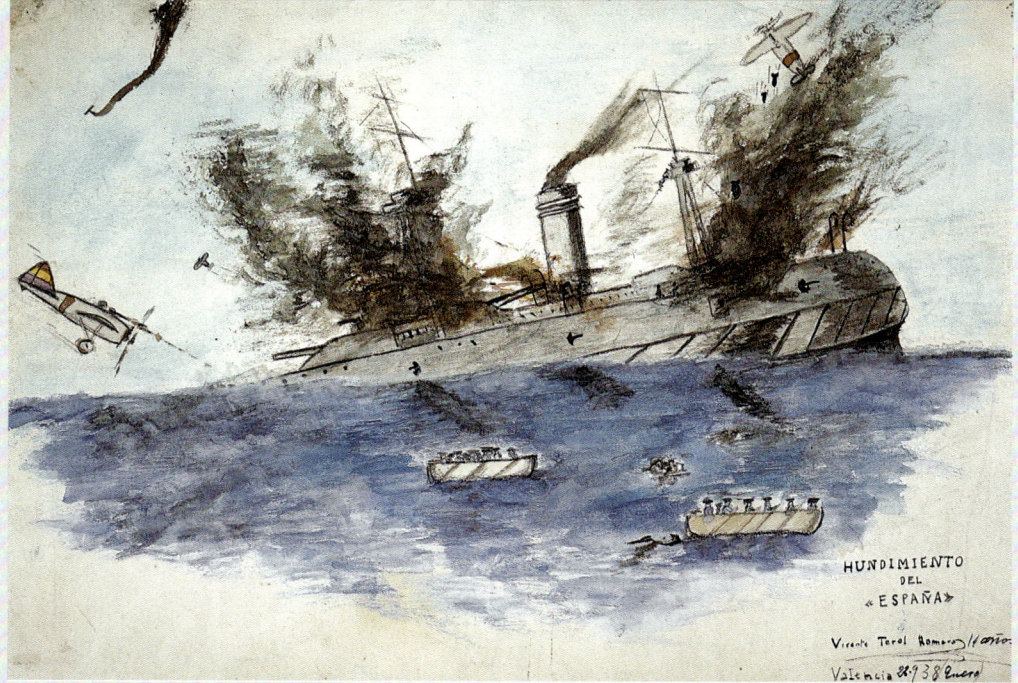

61 WAR

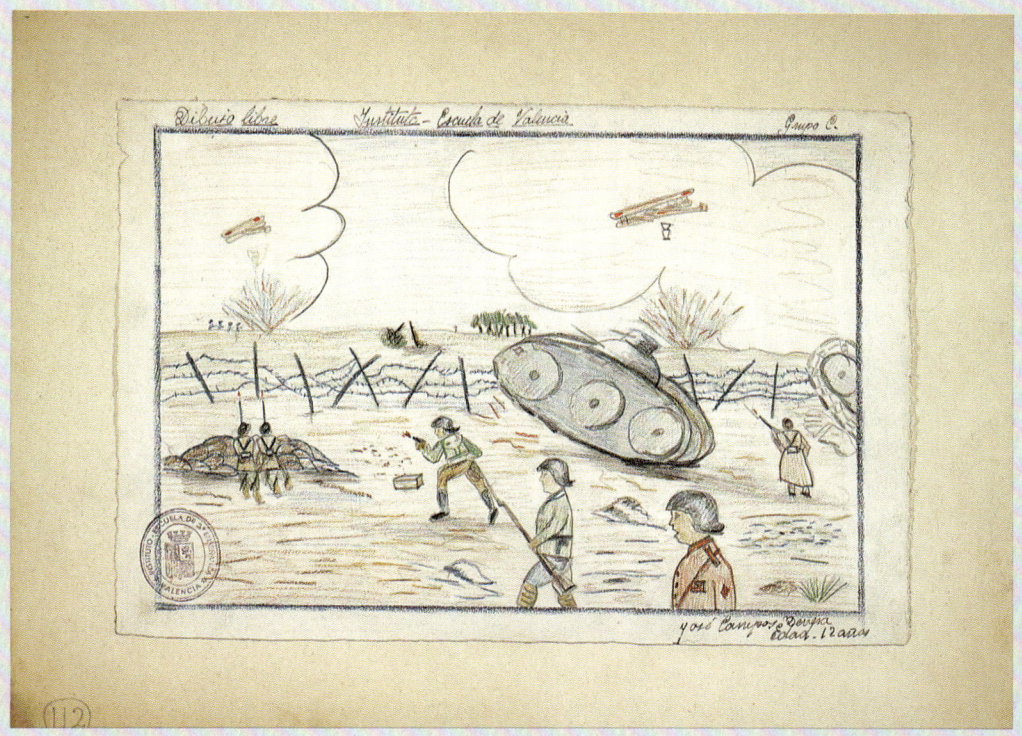

PLATE 14
JOSÉ CAMPOS DEVESA
AGE 12
INSTITUTO-ESCUELA DE 2º
ENSEÑANZA, VALENCIA
"FREE DRAWING"

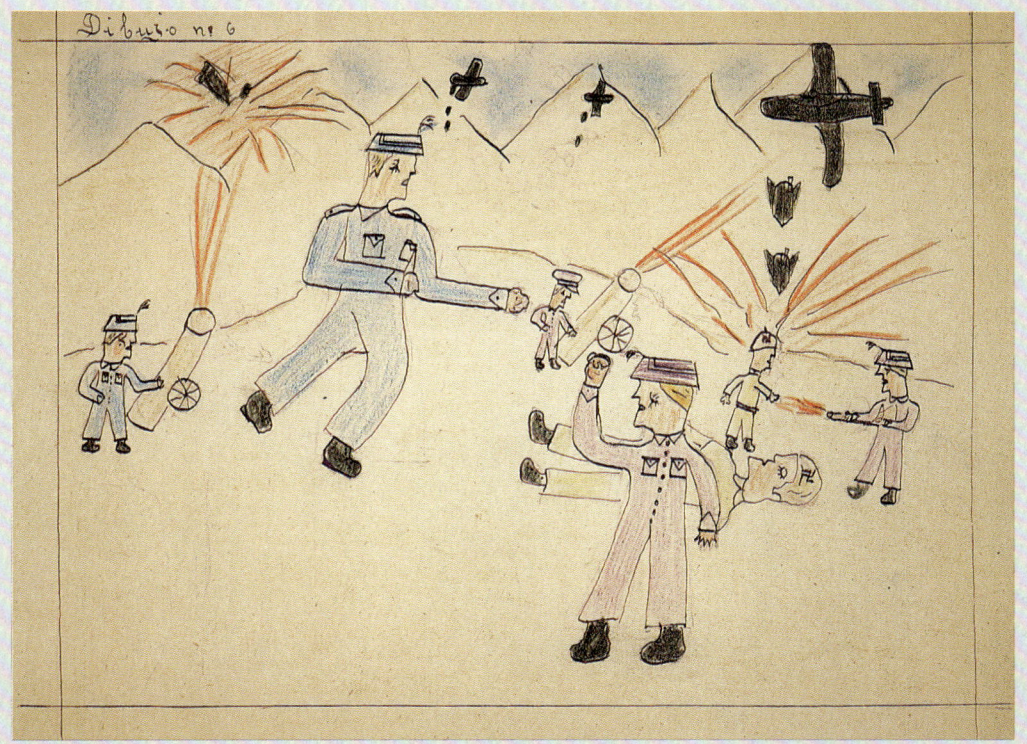

PLATE 15
CONCHITA MUÑOZ JIMÉNEZ
AGE 12
CENTRO ESPAÑOL CERBÈRE (FRANCE)
VERSO: "THIS DRAWING SHOWS THE MILITIAMEN WHO ARE AT THE FRONT, AND WHO ATTACK THE FASCIST AIRPLANES."

62 WAR

PLATE 16
ARTIST UNKNOWN
AGE UNKNOWN
UNIDENTIFIED LOCALE

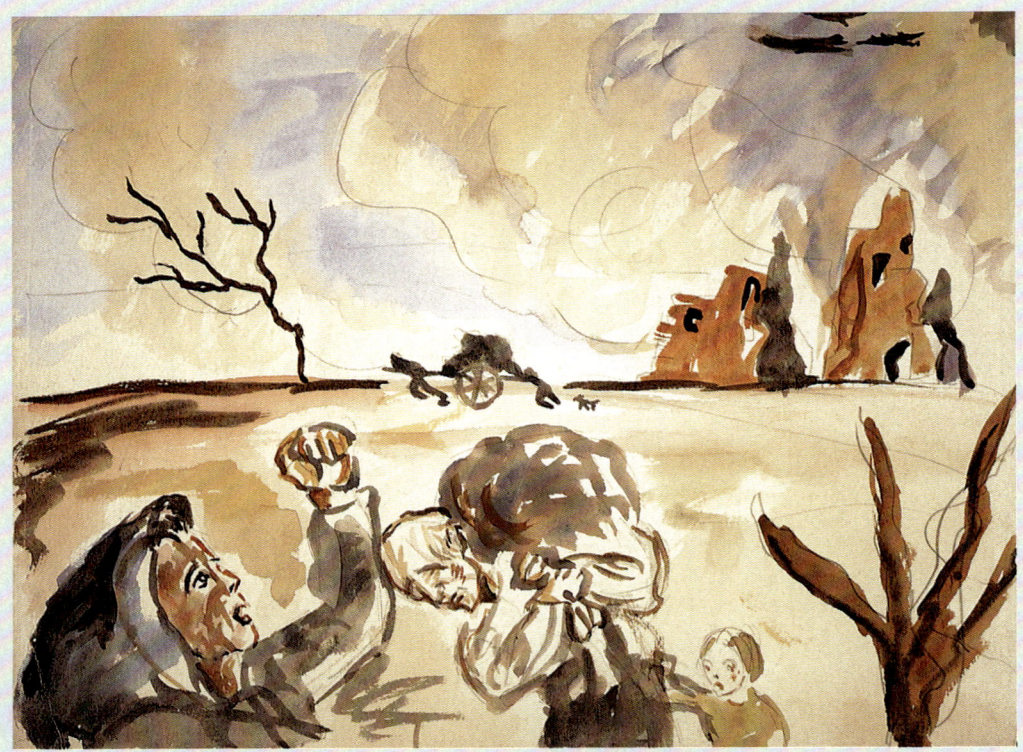

PLATE 17
ALEJANDRO LAZCANO
AGE UNKNOWN
UNIDENTIFIED LOCALE

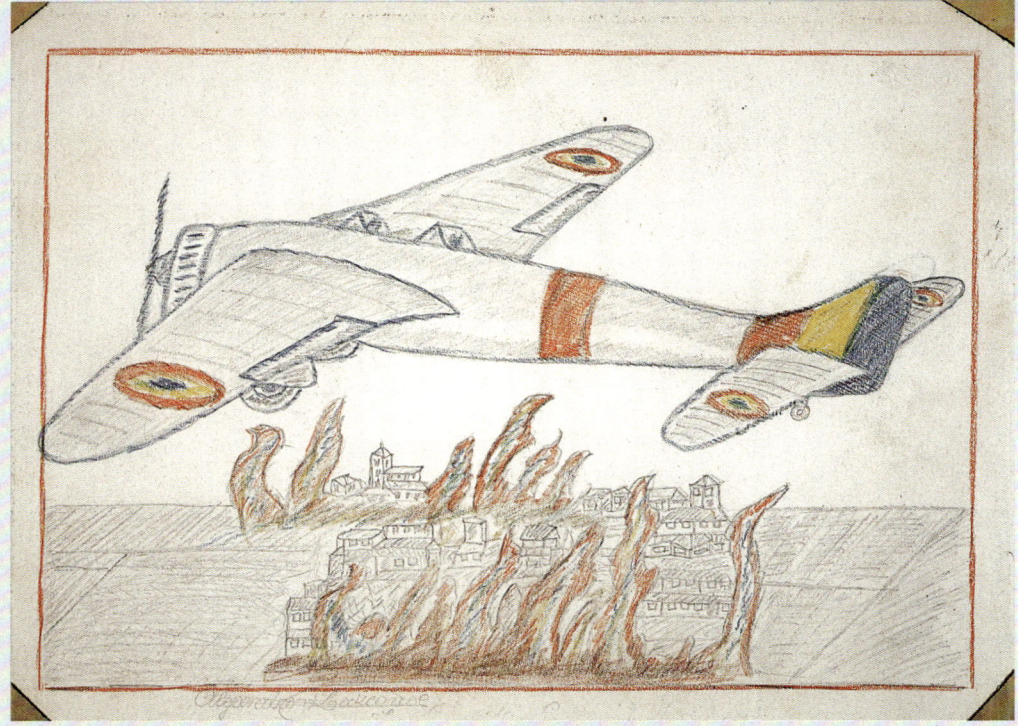

WAR

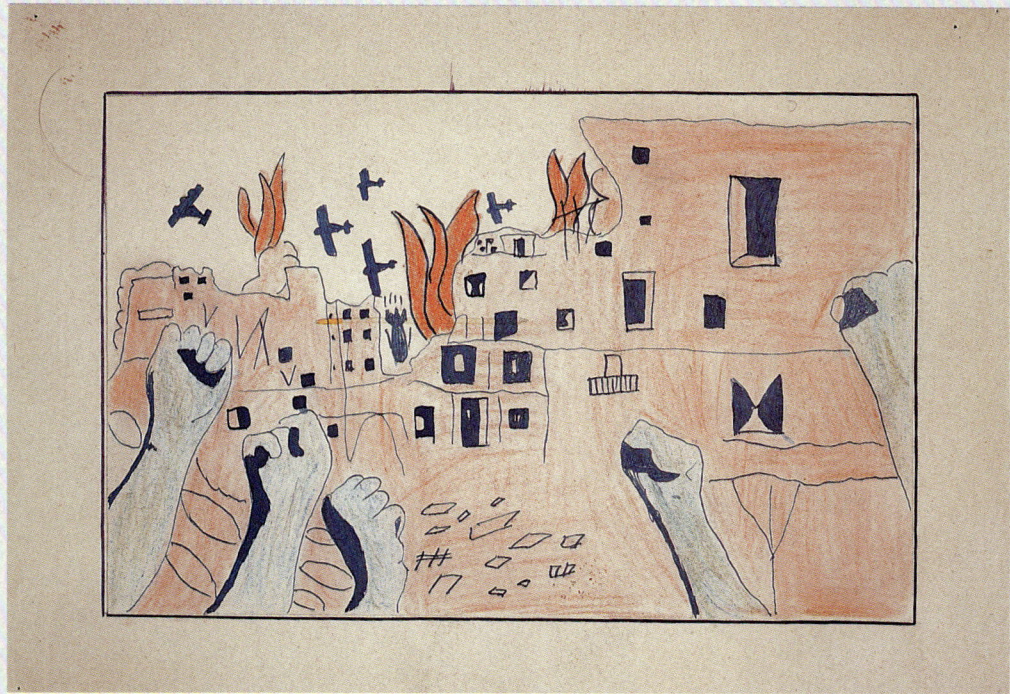

PLATE 18
JUAN APARICIO ALONSO
AGE 12
MINISTERIO DE INSTRUCCIÓN PÚBLICA, ESCUELA-HOGAR ANTELLA (VALENCIA)

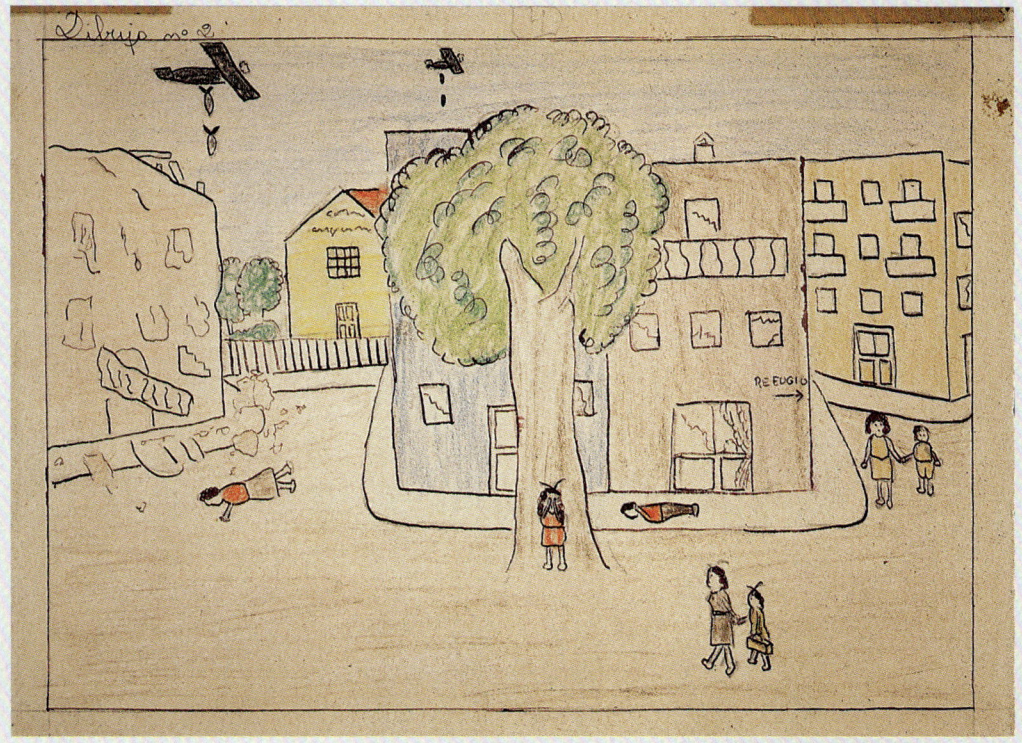

PLATE 19
MARÍA DOLORES SANZ
AGE 13
CENTRO ESPAÑOL CERBÈRE (FRANCE)
VERSO: "THIS SCENE SHOWS A BOMBING IN MY TOWN, PORT-BOU."

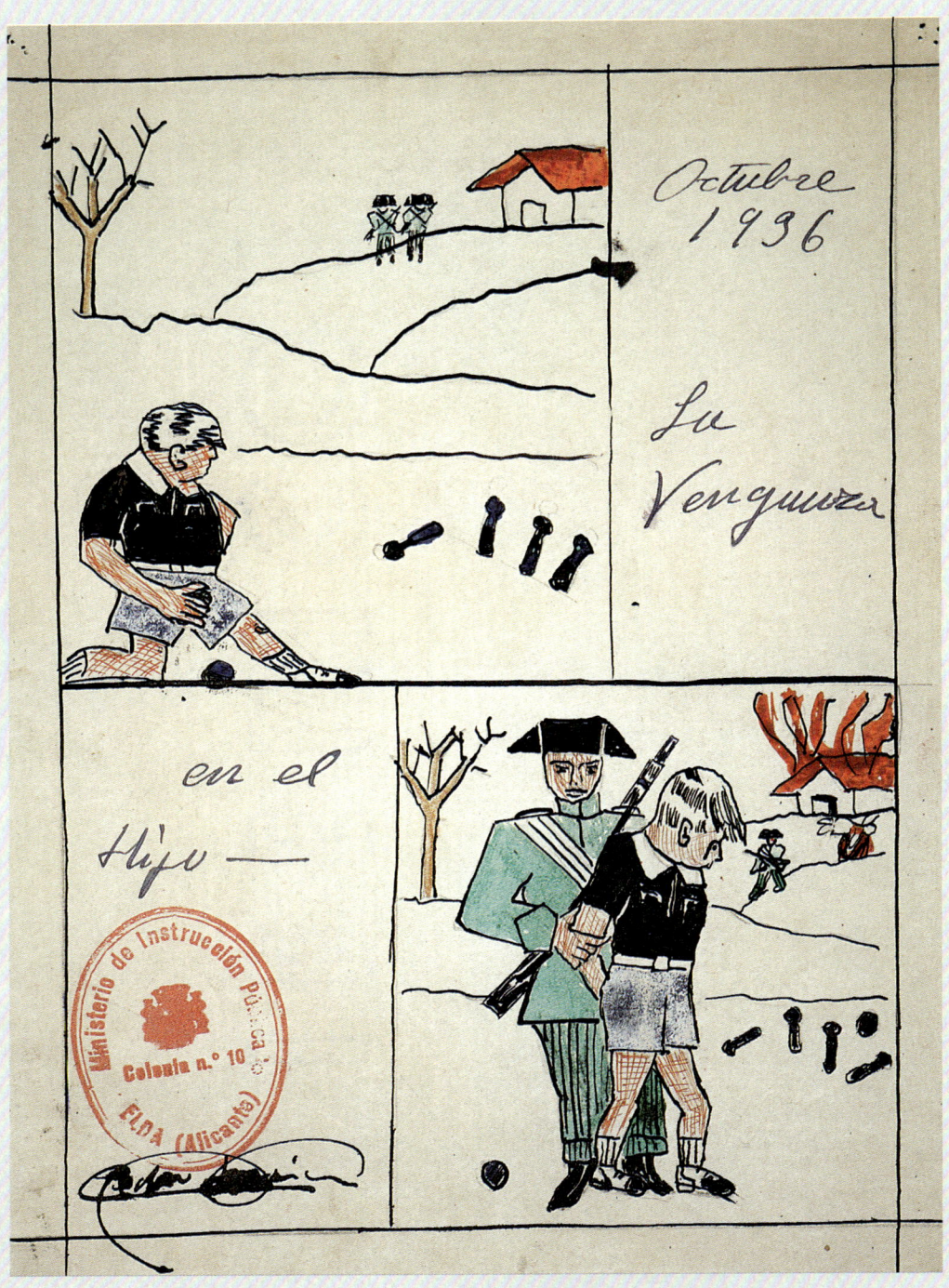

PLATE 20
ARTIST UNKNOWN
AGE UNKNOWN
MINISTERIO DE
INSTRUCCIÓN PÚBLICA,
COLONIA Nº 10
ELDA (ALICANTE)
"REVENGE...ON THE CHILD"

WAR

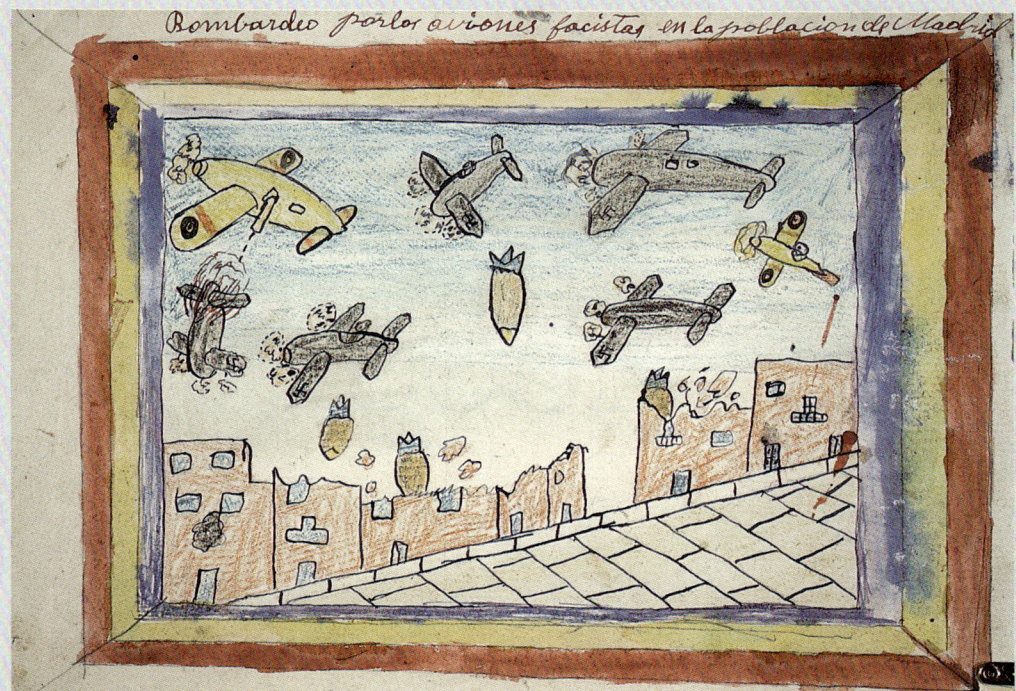

PLATE 21
RAFAEL CERRILLO DOBAL
AGE 13
COLONIA ESCOLAR
GERMÁN ARAUDO
ALCAÑIZ (TERUEL)
"BOMBARDMENT BY FASCIST AIRPLANES ON THE CITY OF MADRID"

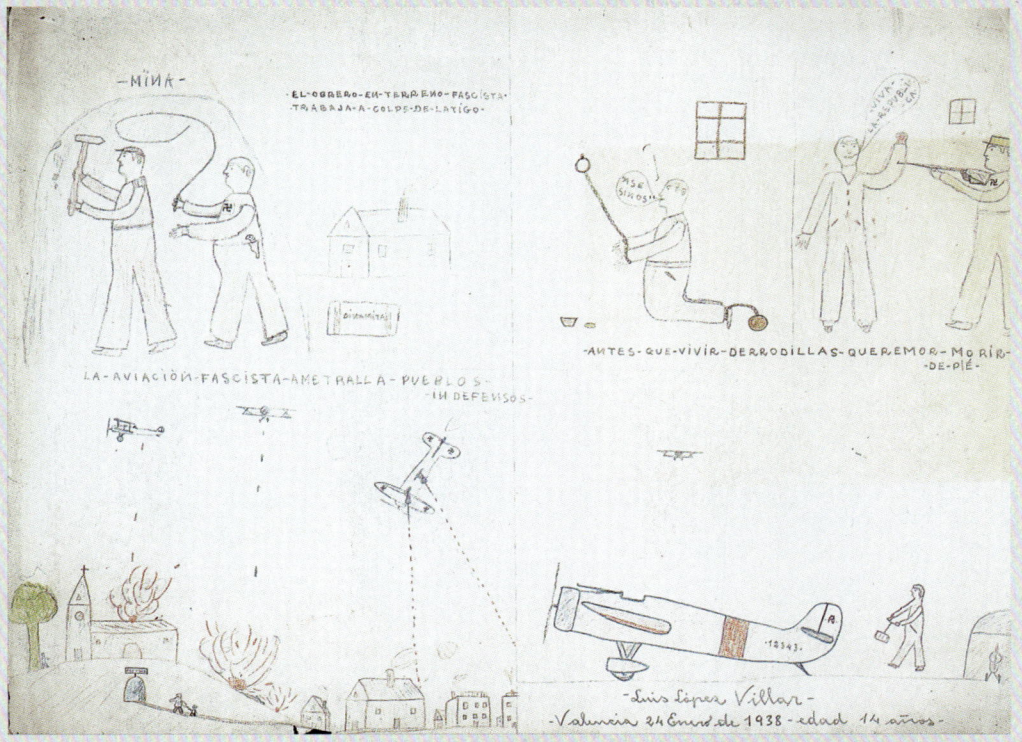

PLATE 22
LUIS LÓPEZ VILLAR
AGE 14
VALENCIA
JANUARY 24, 1938
"MINE. THE WORKER IN FASCIST LANDS WORKS WITH THE CRACK OF A WHIP. THE FASCIST AIRFORCE FIRES SHRAPNEL AT DEFENSELESS TOWNS. BEFORE LIVING ON OUR KNEES WE WANT TO DIE ON OUR FEET. 'ASSASSINS.' 'LONG LIVE THE REPUBLIC.'"

PLATE 23
MAURICIO COLLADOS GARCÍA
AGE 11
CENTRO ESPAÑOL CERBÈRE (FRANCE)
VERSO: "THIS SHOWS MY TOWN, WHEN THE PLANES BOMBED THE UPPER PLAZA AND I RAN FOR THE SHELTER."

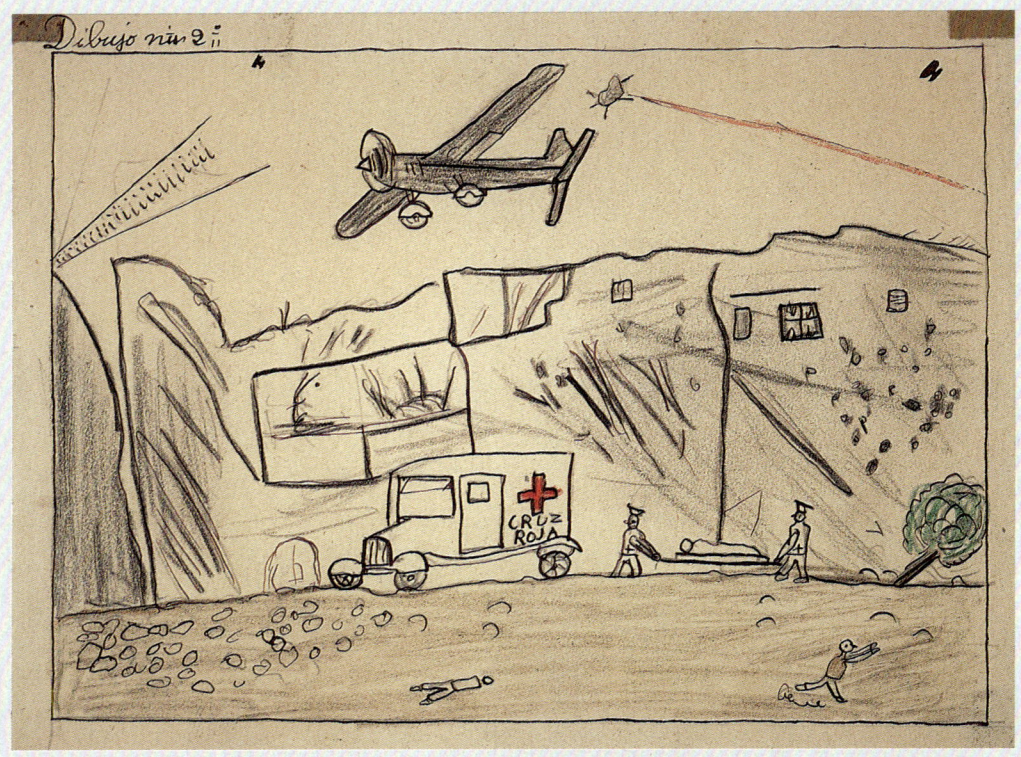

PLATE 24
CONCEPCIÓN RODRÍGUEZ
AGE 13
MASARROCHOS (VALENCIA)
"CONSEQUENCES OF WAR"
"DEATH OF A HERO AND A MOTHER'S GRIEF"

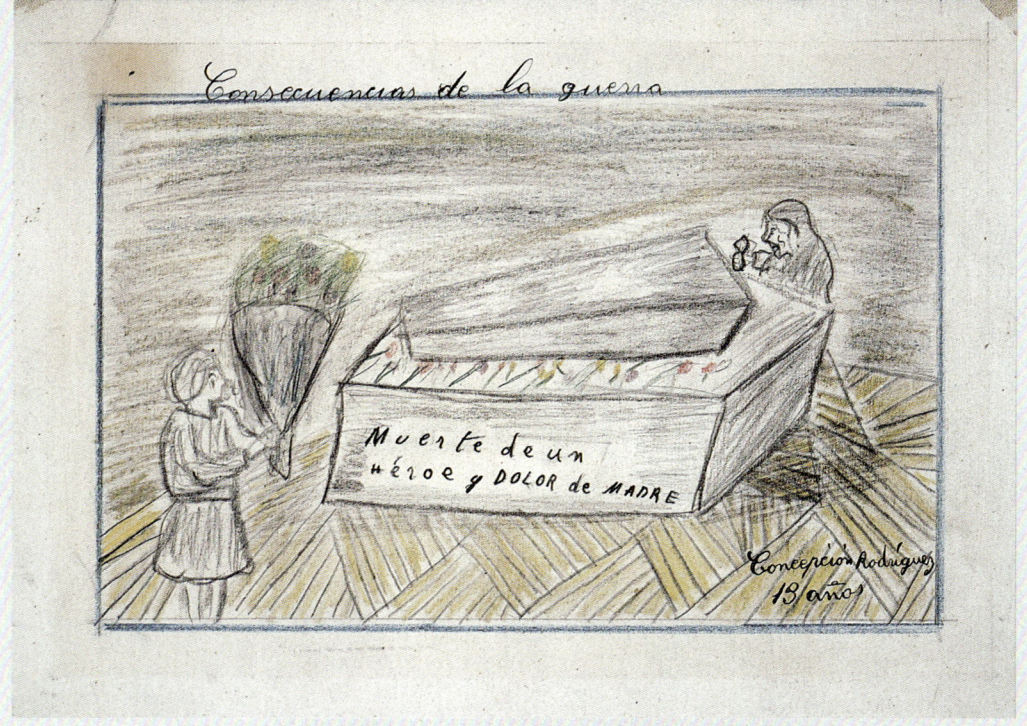

WAR

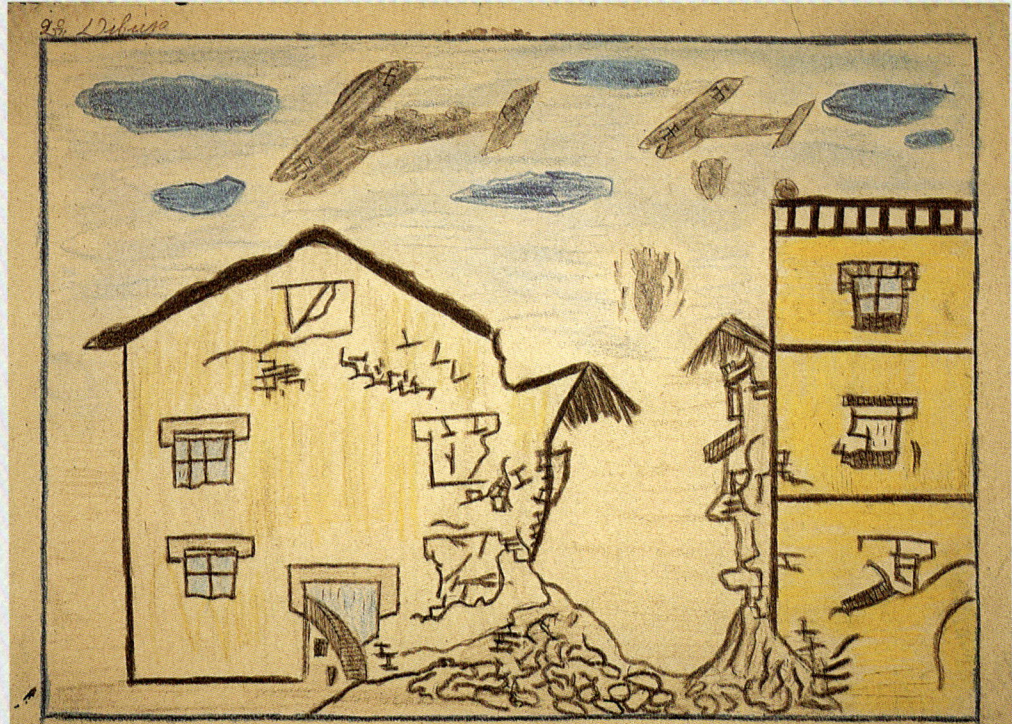

PLATE 25
FILOMENA TORROELLA
AGE 14
CENTRO ESPAÑOL CERBÉRE (FRANCE)
VERSO: "THIS DRAWING SHOWS ONE OF THE HOUSES BLOWN UP BY THE FASCISTS IN PORT-BOU."

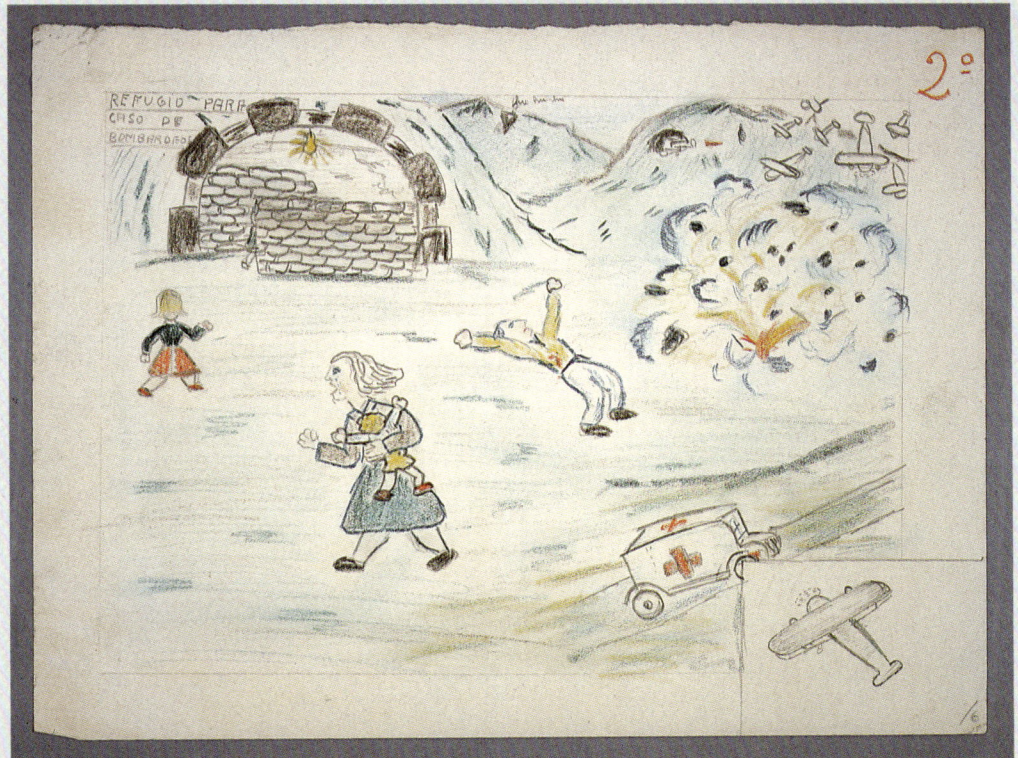

PLATE 26
ARTIST UNKNOWN
AGE UNKNOWN
UNIDENTIFIED LOCALE
"BOMB SHELTER"

DISPLACEMENT

PLATE 27
MARGARITA GARCÍA
AGE 10
RESIDENCIA INFANTIL Nº 23
BIAR (ALICANTE)
"EVACUATION"

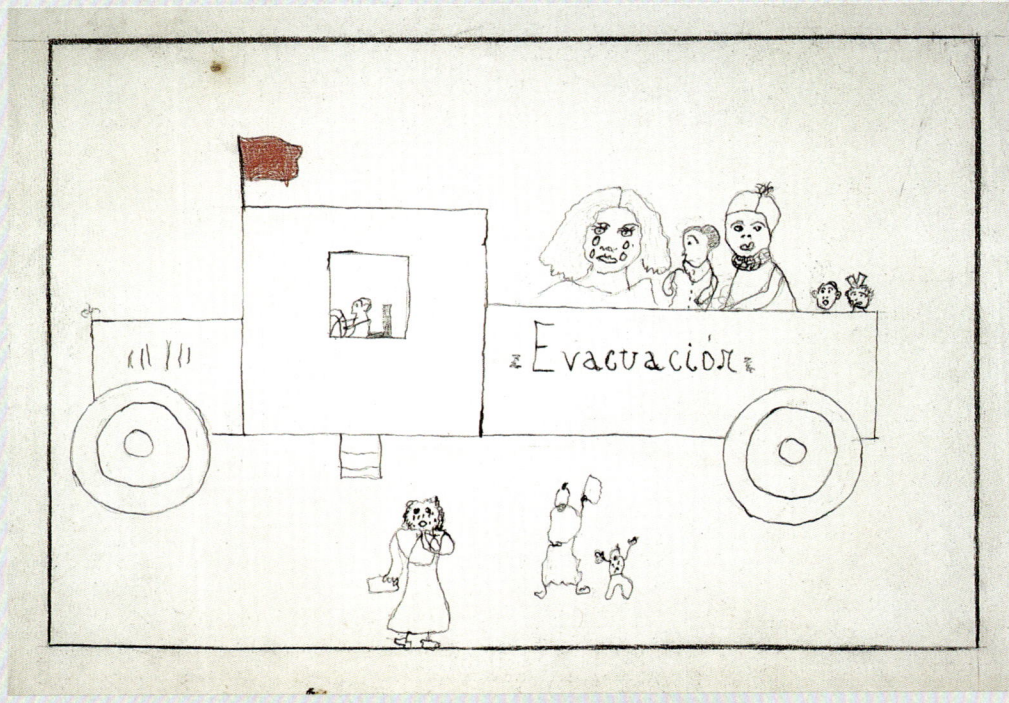

PLATE 28
LUISA RODRÍGUEZ
AGE 11
FROM BILBAO
COLONIA INFANTIL DE BAYONA (FRANCE)
VERSO: "THIS DRAWING IS THE EVACUATION OF MY MOTHER MY BROTHER AND ME AS WE WERE LEAVING FOR SANTANDER. AND THE CANNONS SHOT SHELLS THAT SET MT. ARRAIZ ON FIRE."

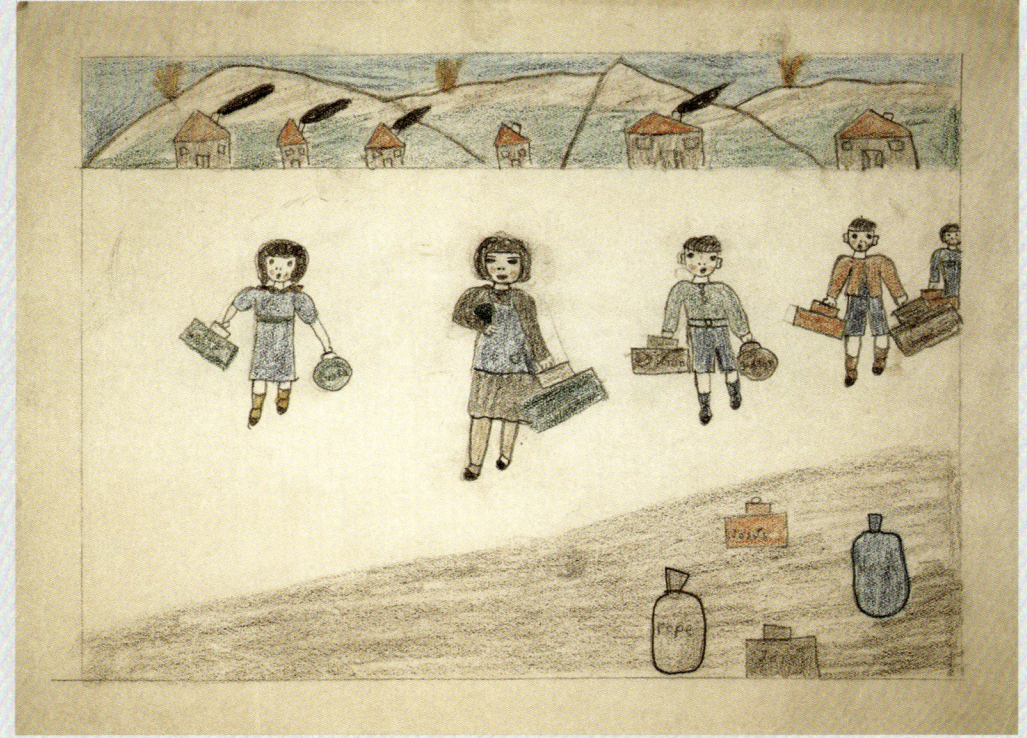

DISPLACEMENT

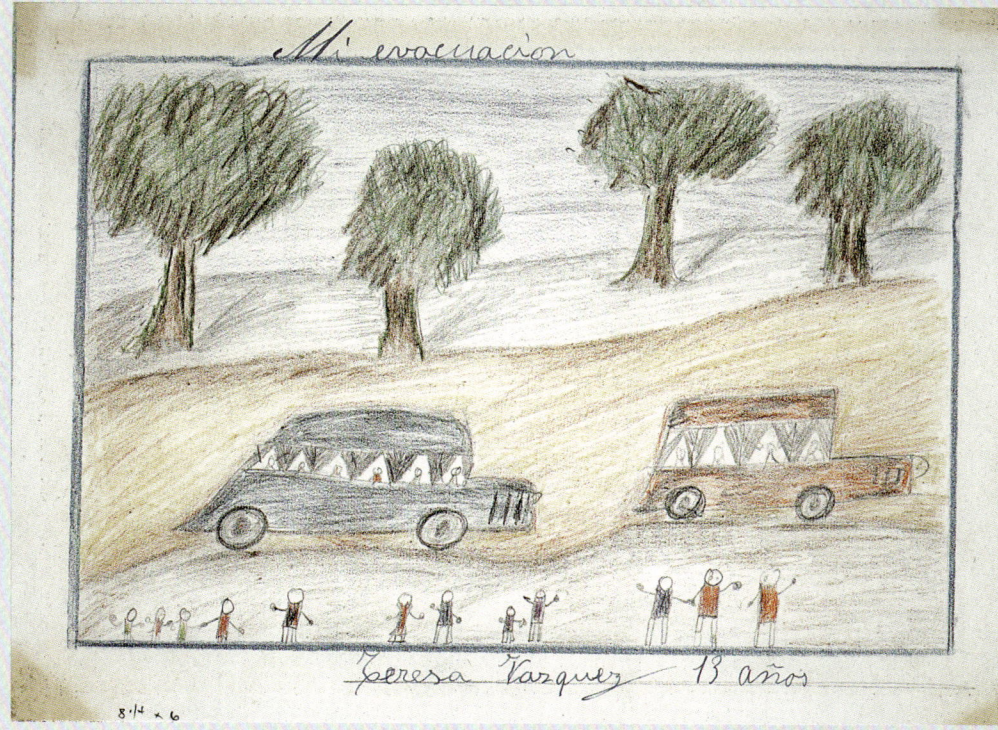

PLATE 29
TERESA VÁZQUEZ
AGE 13
UNIDENTIFIED LOCALE
"MY EVACUATION"

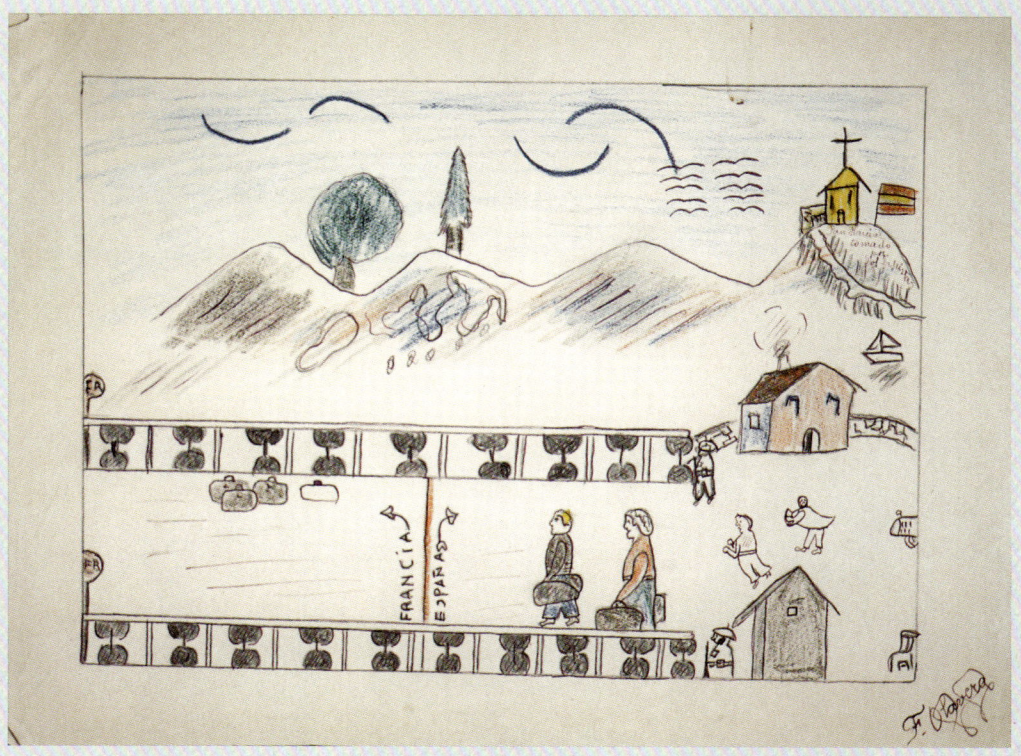

PLATE 30
FERNANDO OLAVERA
AGE 13
COLONIA INFANTIL DE BAYONA (FRANCE):
"SAN MARCIAL TAKEN BY THE FASCISTS"
VERSO: "EVACUATION FROM IRÚN (GUIPUZCOA) DURING THE WAR"

DISPLACEMENT

PLATE 31
MIGUEL ÁNGEL CASTILLO
AGE 8
MINISTERIO DE INSTRUCCIÓN PÚBLICA, COLONIA ESCOLAR Nº 1
TORRENTE (VALENCIA)

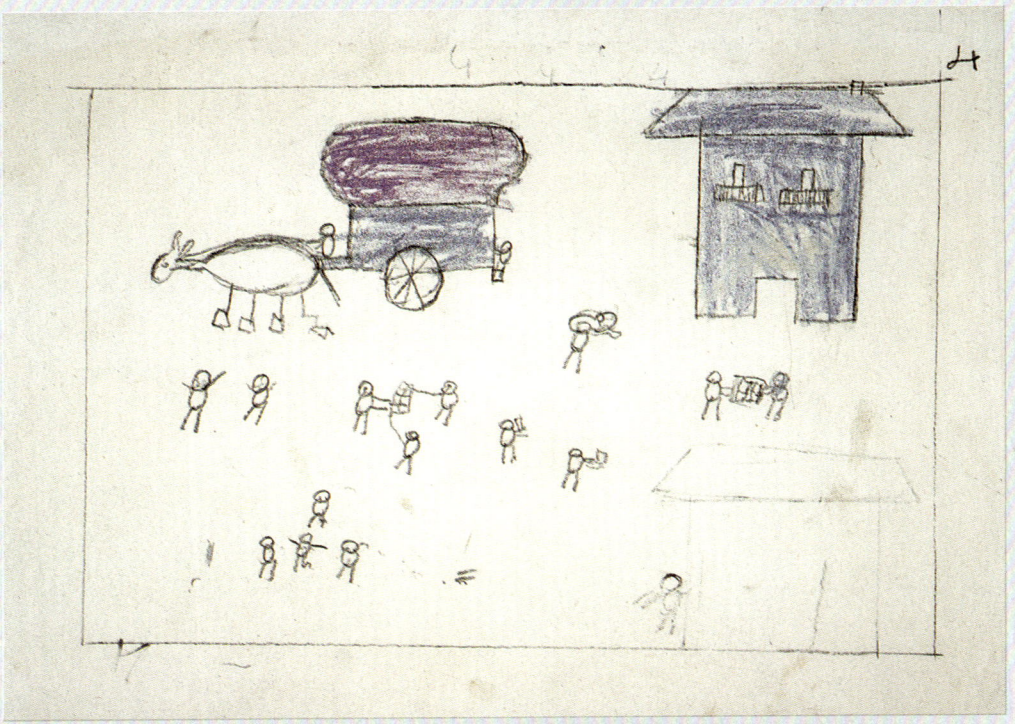

PLATE 32
RESURRECCIÓN RODRÍGUEZ
AGE 11
UNIDENTIFIED LOCALE
"AN EVACUATION"

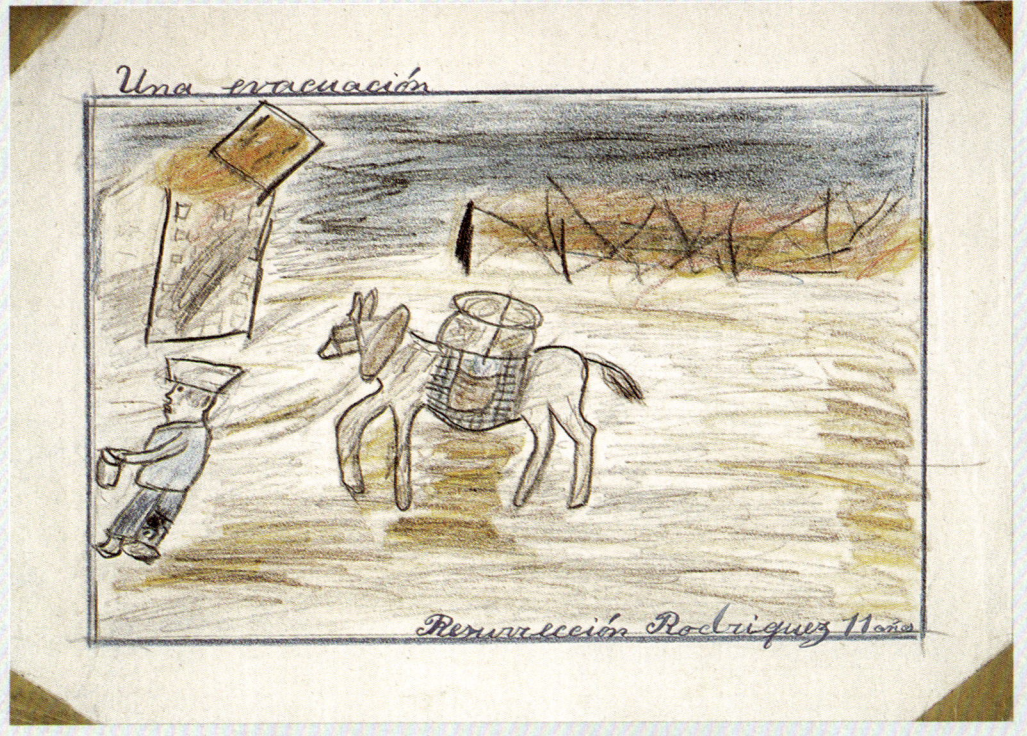

DISPLACEMENT

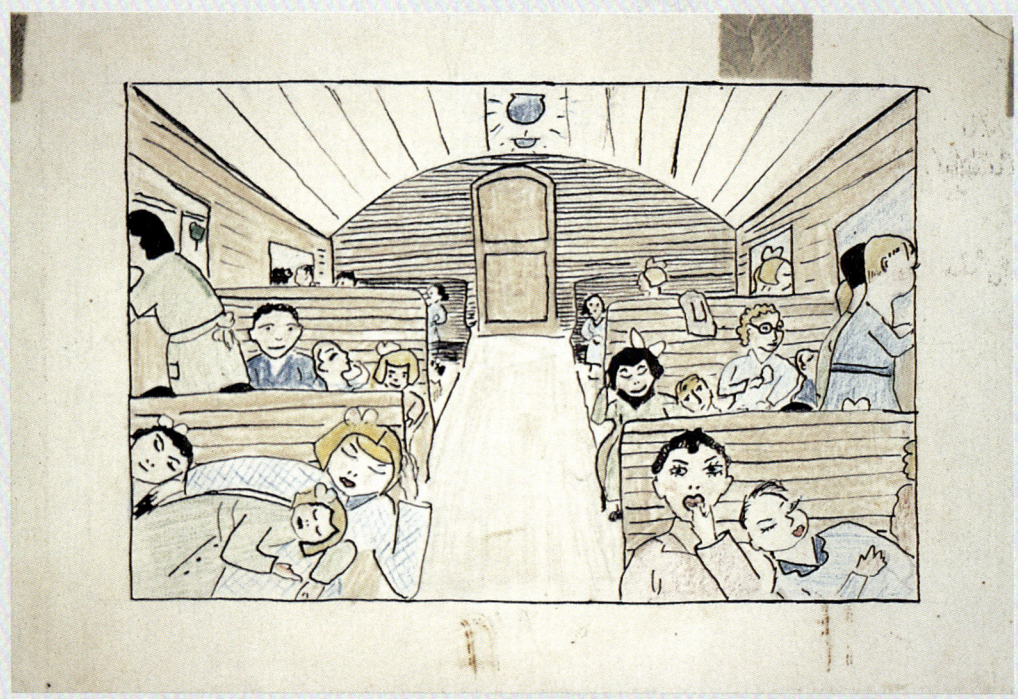

PLATE 33
RAFAELA JOVER RODRÍGUEZ
AGE 13
COLONIA ESCOLAR BELLÚS (VALENCIA)
VERSO: "DURING THE TRIP"

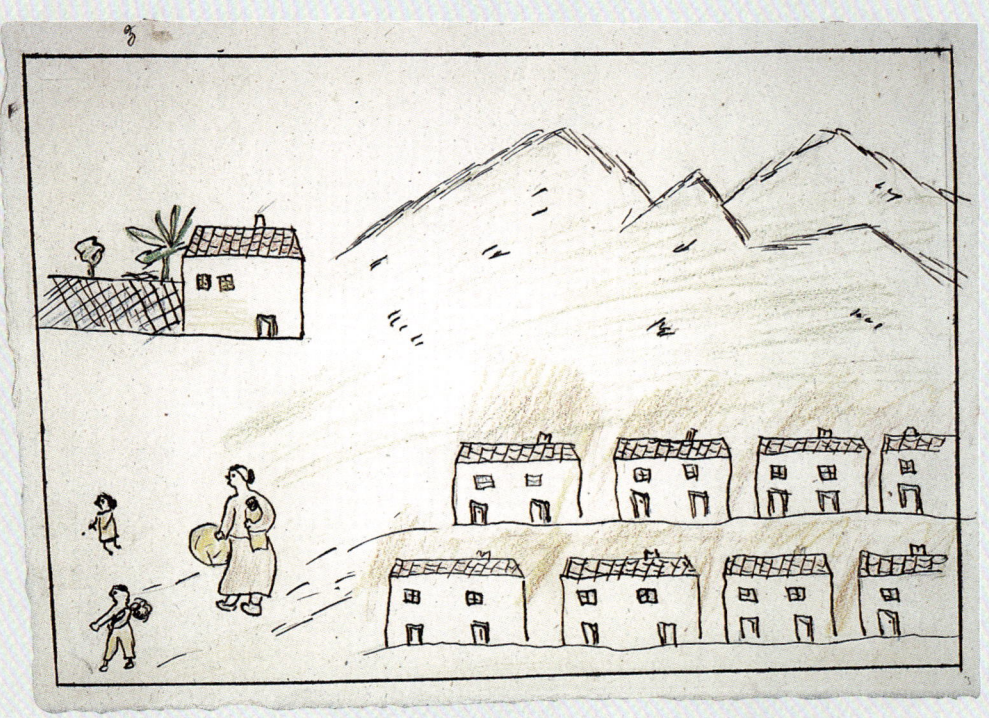

PLATE 34
FRANCISCA MÁRQUEZ MARTÍNEZ
AGE 13
GUARDERÍA INFANTIL DE GUERRA, TRABAJADORES DE LA ENSEÑANZA, UGT
LOBOSILLO (MURCIA)

CAMPS

PLATE 35
JESÚS EZQUERRO RUIZ
AGE 10
RESIDENCIA INFANTIL Nº 1
ONTENIENTE (VALENCIA)
"THE CHILD IN THE COLONY"

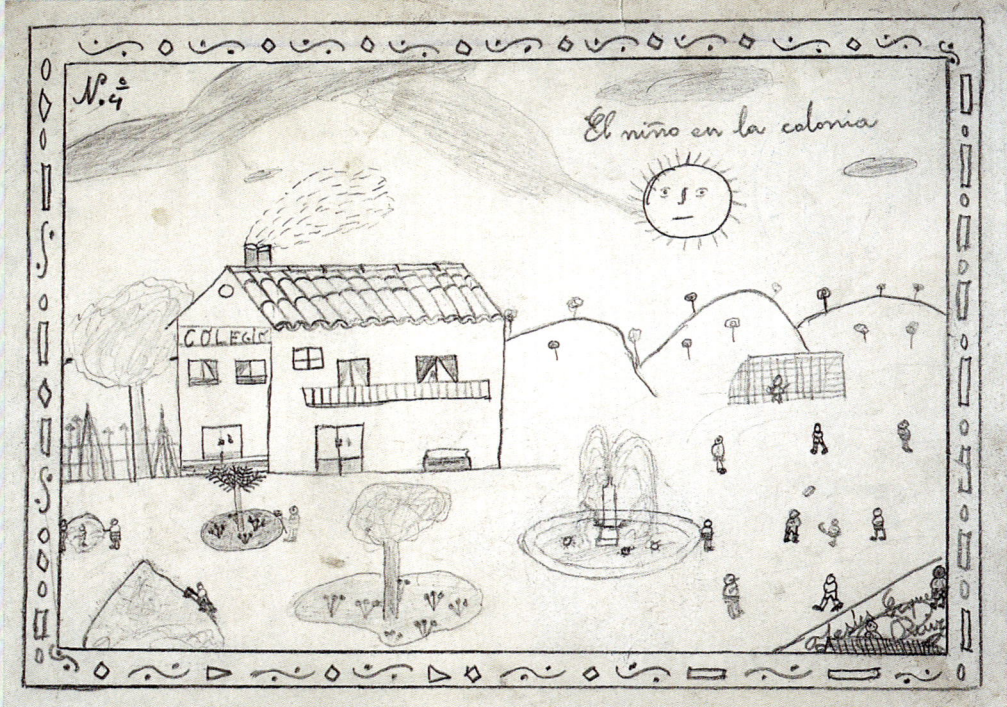

PLATE 36
NATALIO GÓMEZ MARTÍN
AGE 14
RESIDENCIA INFANTIL Nº 14
MONFORTE DEL CID (ALICANTE)
"LIFE IN THE COLONY"

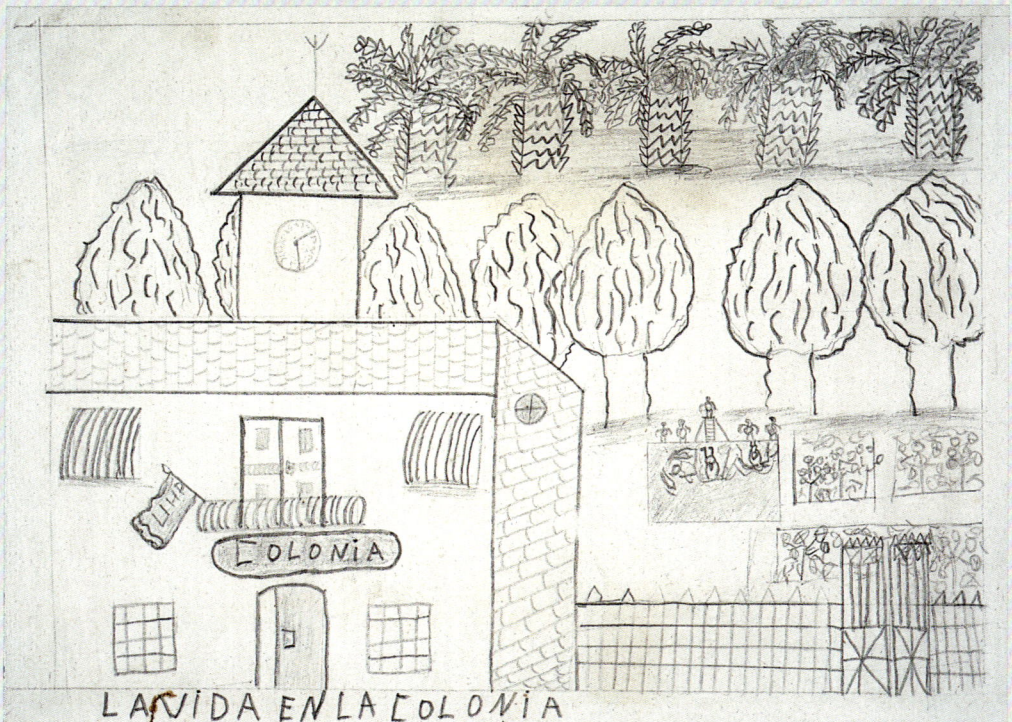

CAMPS

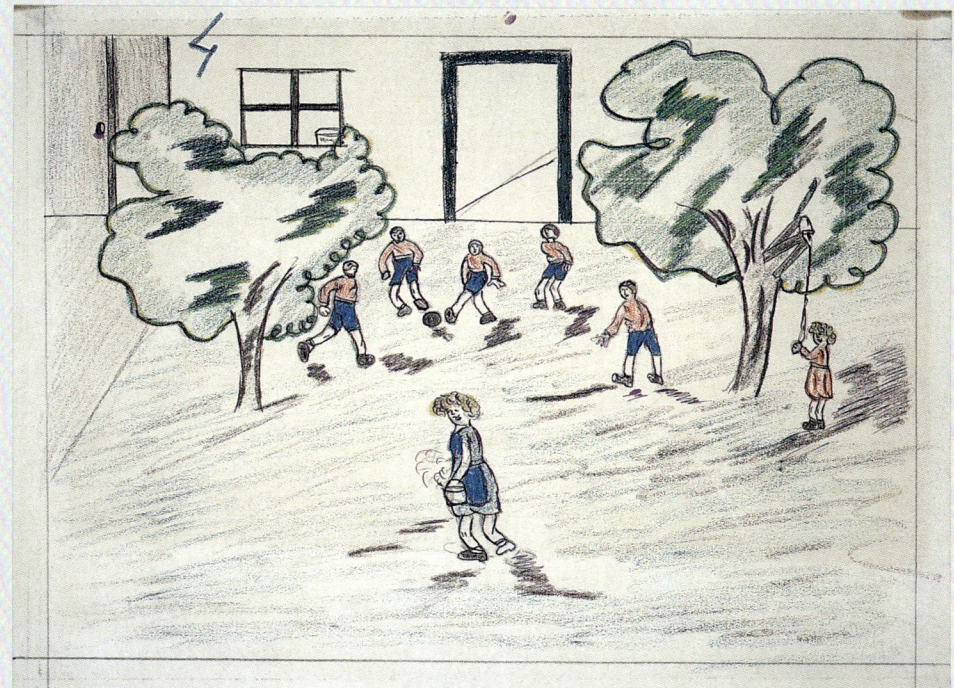

PLATE 37
ÁNGELES ARNÁIZ
AGE 14
COLONIA INFANTIL DE BAYONA (FRANCE)
VERSO: "I DID THIS DRAWING TO SHOW OUR LIFE IN THE COLONY, HERE WE SEE SOME BOYS PLAYING BALL, ANOTHER ONE WHO IS ME RINGING THE BELL BECAUSE IT IS TIME TO EAT, AND THE COOK CARRYING THE POT OF FOOD."

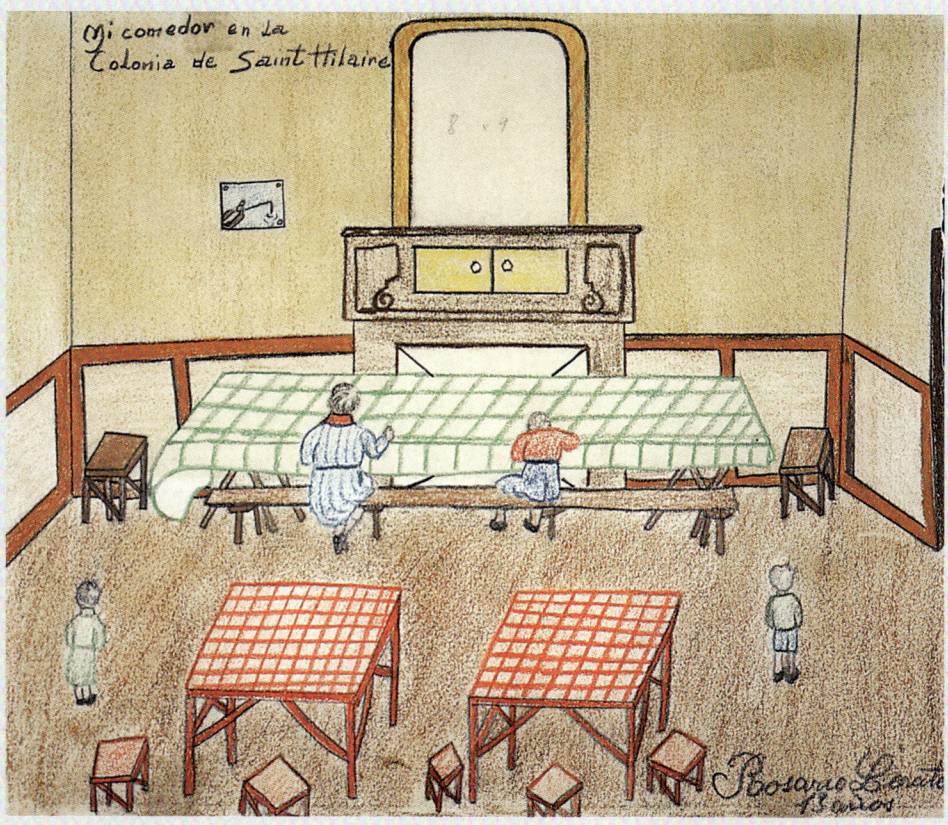

PLATE 38
ROSARIO LORATE
AGE 13
COLONIA DE SAINT-HILAIRE (FRANCE)
"MY DINING ROOM IN THE COLONY IN SAINT-HILAIRE"

PEACE

PLATE 39
CARMEN SIERRA
AGE 12
MINISTERIO DE
INSTRUCCIÓN PÚBLICA,
RESIDENCIA INFANTIL Nº 20
TANGEL (ALICANTE)

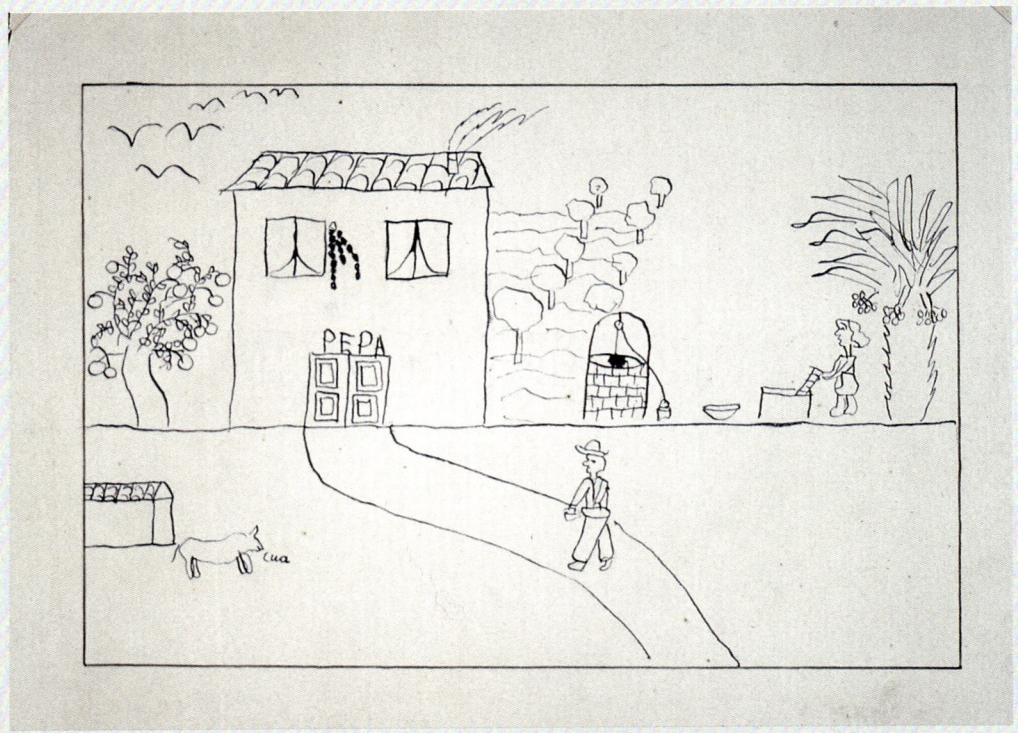

PLATE 40
EMILIO DÍAZ LUNA
AGE 9
MASARROCHOS (VALENCIA)
"MASONS WORKING.
I WILL BE A MASON."
VERSO: "AFTER THE WAR"

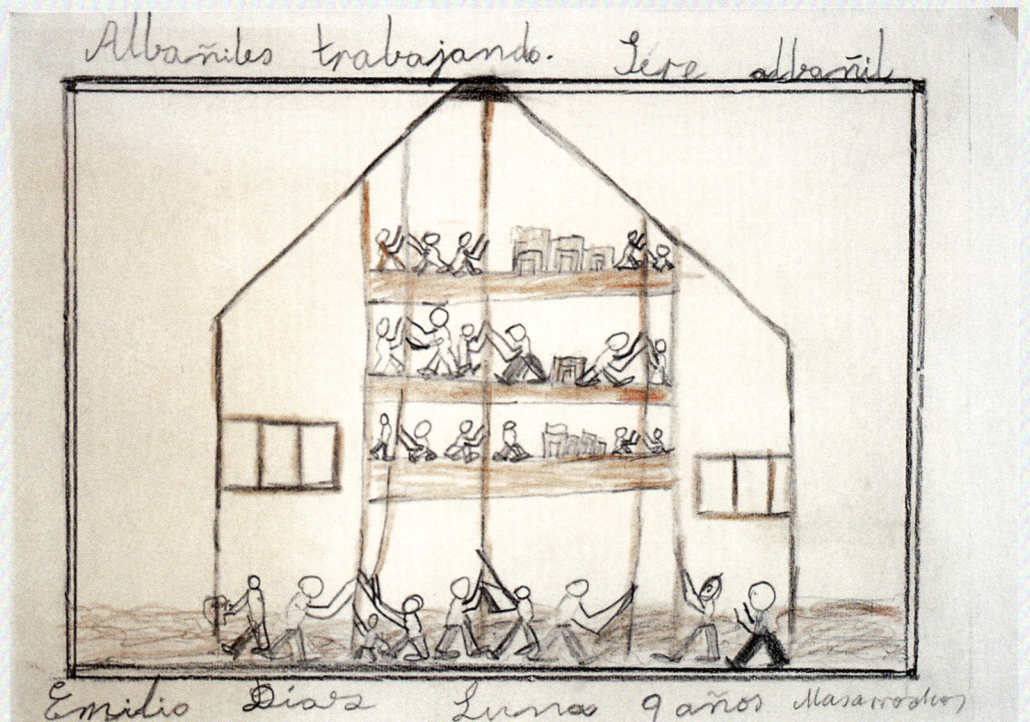

PEACE

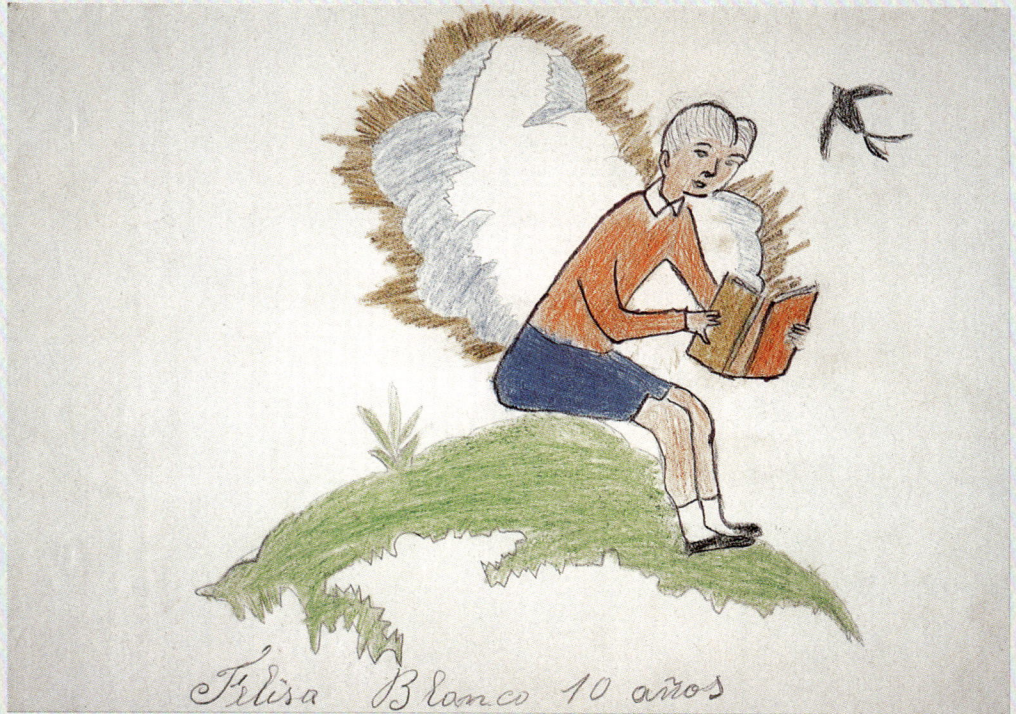

PLATE 41
FELISA BLANCO
AGE 10
ESCUELA NACIONAL DE NIÑAS, MADRID

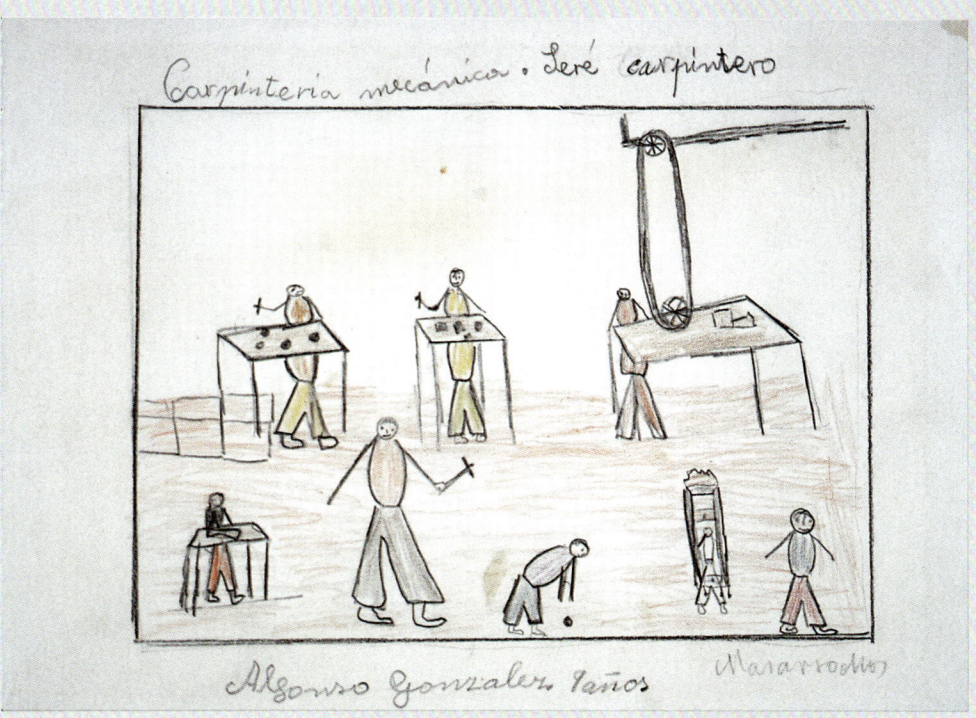

PLATE 42
ALFONSO GONZÁLEZ
AGE 9
MASARROCHOS (VALENCIA)
"MECHANICAL CARPENTRY. I WILL BE A CARPENTER."
VERSO: "AFTER THE WAR"

PLATE 43
ALFONSO ORTUÑO
AGE 11

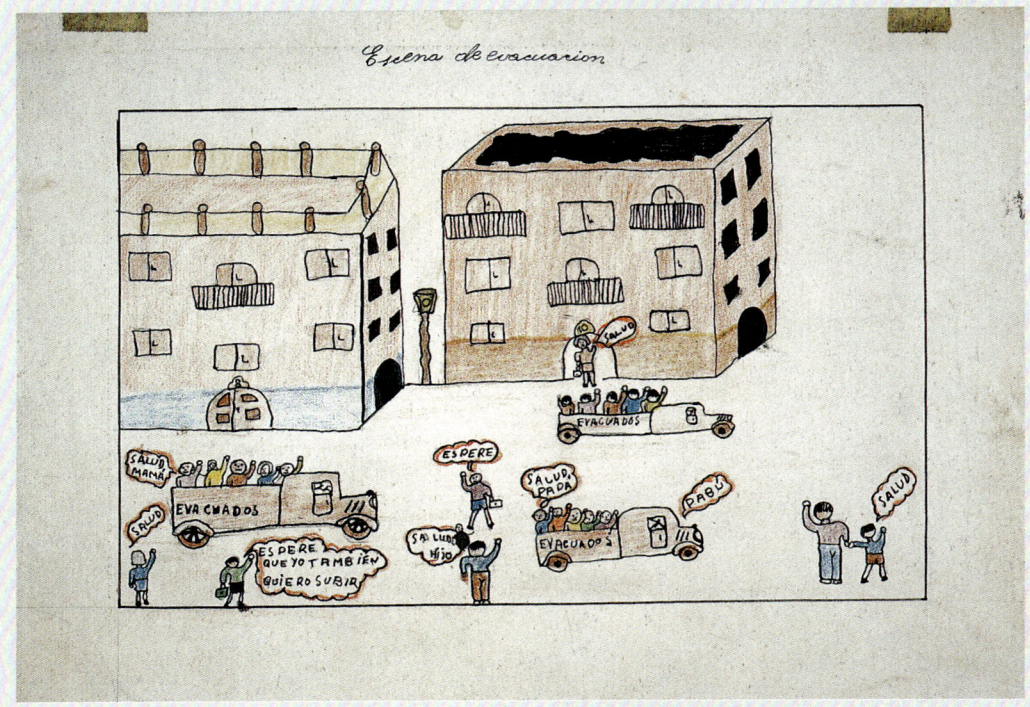

"I LOVED DRAWING, I DREW HUNDREDS OF PICTURES, AND PROBABLY SOMEONE TOLD ME TO DRAW WHAT I HAD SEEN IN MADRID. AND THIS IS WHAT I SAW, THE EVACUATION, WHAT I REMEMBERED BEFORE BEING EVACUATED. I REMEMBER THEY SAID GOOD-BYE SAYING 'SALUD, SALUD' BECAUSE THE WORD 'DIOS' (GOD, AS IN 'ADIÓS') WASN'T USED THEN, IT HAD BEEN ELIMINATED IN THE REPUBLICAN ZONE."

ALFONSO ORTUÑO
AGE 76
BORN IN MADRID
RETIRED WOOD CARVER

INTERVIEW

ALFONSO ORTUÑO, MARCH 8, 2001, MADRID

DO YOU HAVE ANY MEMORIES OF THE WAR IN MADRID?

I remember the terror my mother felt when the sirens sounded and the *"pavas"* came; that's what we called the German airplanes that bombed the city, "turkeys." Most of the neighbors came to our apartment, which was on a lower floor, and my mother nearly fainted, and with terror in her body she hugged my sister and me tight until the bombardment was over. My mother couldn't stand it, and so she must have thought that it was best to send her kids to safety, knowing what it means for a parent to send her children away.

WHAT DO YOU REMEMBER ABOUT YOUR EVACUATION FROM MADRID?

In Madrid I went to the Miguel de Unamuno public school, in the Embajadores neighborhood. And I remember that in September 1936 they had a meeting with the students' parents. I noticed that when the meeting was over many of the mothers had tears in their eyes. How strange, I thought, how strange. Of course, it wasn't long before I found out why they were crying. They had proposed to all the parents that those who wanted could send their children out of Madrid to parts of Spain less punished by the war. And my parents signed up me and my sister (my sister was two years older than me).

I remember that we left on October 1, 1936. I was ten years old. They told us we were going to live in *colonias*, in camps, which turned out not to be the case. We went to Valencia on a train with about 100 kids and some teachers who chaperoned us. When we got to Valencia they gave us a sandwich. After about two hours they took us to another train station, and from there to a town called Puebla Larga, between Carcagente and Játiva.

In Játiva there was a town crier who had alerted the citizens of Puebla Larga that the children were arriving and that those who were willing should take us in until the war ended and we could go home. They took us to a building called the Casa del Pueblo. I remember this perfectly. The people of this town were waiting there, and they chose us like slaves: "I want this one, I don't want that one.... I'll take this one, I'll leave that one...." Like slaves.

I think they sent us to Valencia first so our parents would be comforted thinking they were taking us to *colonias*, but that's not what happened. They put us there like slaves on the block, and it was heartbreaking. That experience left its mark on me and I'll never forget it: "I'll take this one, I won't take that one...," heartbreaking. It is forever engraved in my memory. That and the town crier, because I had never seen a town crier and didn't even know what they were.

WHAT HAPPENED THAT FIRST NIGHT?

I remember that my sister was crying, because we had never been separated, and she clung to me and wouldn't let go. Then there was this couple that was interested in taking either me or my sister. A couple from that town. But we were holding each other so tight that it was impossible to tear us apart: they had to take both of us or neither. Poor things, may they rest in peace. They were very good people and had no choice but to take us both. His name was Antonio Rodríguez. And his wife was Julia. They had four children. Truth be told, I am very grateful to them, they treated us like their own children.

INTERVIEW

WERE YOU ABLE TO STAY IN TOUCH WITH YOUR PARENTS?

My mother was poor. It was the first time she had ever been separated from us, and she was sobbing here in Madrid. Completely alone, because my father was working in Catalonia, in Reus, for the company Construcciones Aeronáuticas. And what happened was that my mother couldn't take it, because it was intolerable to be separated from us—she was a lively and witty woman, though illiterate—and two months later she came to Puebla Larga and found work in a café, which was also a pension and restaurant. This way she could see us.

After a while my mother was able to rent a little house right in the same town, and six or seven months later I went to live with her. My sister didn't; she went to live with another family, a certain José Palencia, who had a very good social position and owned lots of land, though she spent more time with my mother and me than with them.

My father sent us money from Reus, and nearly every month he would send us packages of food. When the packages arrived we would celebrate. He sent lentils, rice, sugar.... And since he didn't smoke, he would trade his ration of tobacco for food, to send to us. The days the packages arrived were like holidays, my sister and I were tremendously happy.

DID YOU GO TO SCHOOL?

We went to school there and learned what we could. Our teacher was very old and the kids were all different ages. Life was quite peaceful. We followed the town crier around, swam in the irrigation ditches and ponds. There was no movie theater; we had to go to Carcagente, some 5 kilometers away, if we wanted to see a movie. Puebla Larga was clearly not a military target because the air raid shelter was never used, and the whole time we were there only three bombs were dropped on the train station. They didn't explode and were stuck in the ground by the tracks.

WHAT HAPPENED WHEN THE WAR ENDED?

When we moved back to Madrid I was thirteen and there was nothing but hunger in Madrid. In Valencia we never went hungry. There was never an overabundance of food, but we always had rice. And if there was no bread they made cornmeal biscuits, and that's what we ate.

On the way back, it took us three days to get there, because the train stopped at every little town and it took forever. We even ran out of food and the women got out at one station to cook a rice dish and they hadn't finished making the meal when the whistle blew and they had to leave the pots there and jump back on the train. So we were starving when we got to Madrid.

I wept when I was evacuated from Madrid, but I cried just as hard when we left Puebla Larga to return to Madrid.

ALFONSO ORTUÑO

DID YOUR FAMILY SUFFER ANY REPRISALS AFTER THE WAR?

After the war my father went to France and we didn't hear from him for years, we didn't even know if he was dead or alive. Until finally one day we got a letter from him telling us he was in a concentration camp in France, but he was going to come back under an amnesty that Franco offered to exiles who did not have blood on their hands. He returned in 1959, shortly before my mother died. At that time, my wife and I were living abroad with our daughters, but fortunately I was able to come back to Spain to see him.

DID YOU STAY IN TOUCH WITH THE FAMILY THAT TOOK YOU IN?

When I got married in 1952 my wife and I went back to Puebla Larga to see the family I lived with. I had also gone to see them when I was twenty, because I was in the area. They were crazy about my mother. We kept in touch with them until they died.

HOW WOULD YOU EVALUATE YOUR EXPERIENCE OF THE WAR?

Looking back over the years, I am glad that things happened the way they did and that my sister and I were spared the horrors of the war by being evacuated to Puebla Larga. The way my mother suffered when the sirens went off was awful. You could see death in her face. And besides, it was an experience. Maybe because of it I was not afraid to seek work in Holland, Switzerland, and Germany with my wife and two daughters, who went to school in Switzerland.

YOUR DRAWING WILL BE EXHIBITED WITH CHILDREN'S ART FROM LATER WARS. HOW DO YOU FEEL KNOWING THAT CHILDREN STILL SUFFER THE EFFECTS OF WAR?

When I see pictures of children in war today, it brings tears to my eyes. It's hard to believe that this continued into the twentieth century. It's inhuman. So many epidemics, so many diseases, when we've landed on the Moon and we want to go to Mars. With such tremendous wealth in so many countries, to think that there are children suffering such calamities. This wouldn't happen if the rich countries got together and sent money to alleviate this, because God knows there's enough money, but they prefer to spend it on arms. The more money people have, the less compassion they show. ∎

"I AM A PACIFIST ONE HUNDRED PERCENT. WAR IS ATROCIOUS TO ME. IT IS TRAFFICKING IN HUMAN LIVES."

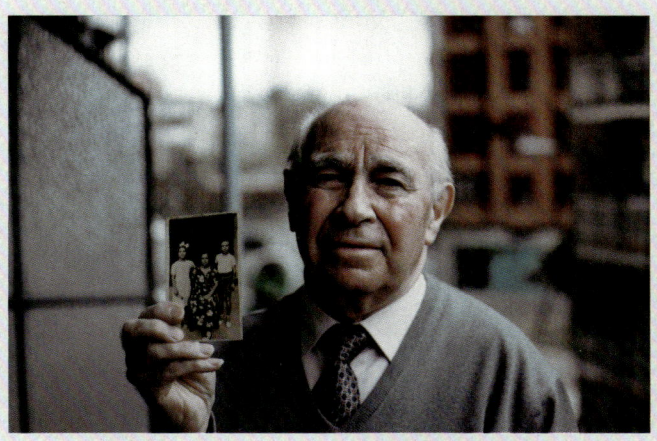

ALFONSO ORTUÑO
AGE 76
IN HIS HAND HE HOLDS A PHOTO OF HIMSELF, WITH HIS MOTHER AND SISTER, TAKEN IN PUEBLA LARGA IN 1938
PHOTOGRAPH BY MIGUEL ÁNGEL NIETO

80

The University of Illinois Press is a founding member of the Association of American University Presses

Composed in Filosofia/Filosofia Grand and FUTURA

Filosofia was designed by Zuzana Licko for Emigre in 1996 based on the design of Bodoni.

FUTURA WAS DESIGNED BY PAUL RENNER IN 1936

Graphic design and typesetting by Sol R. Sender

Manufactured by Friesens Corporation

University of Illinois Press
1325 South Oak Street
Champaign, IL 61820-6903
www.press.uillinois.edu

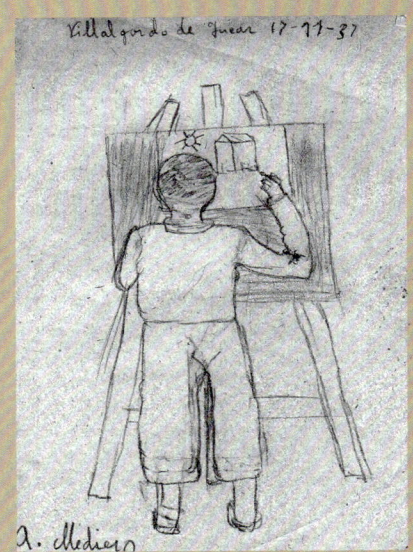

FIGURE 35
A. MEDIERO
AGE UNKNOWN